MW01487495

Moadim LeSimcha
Explorations Into the Jewish Holidays

מועדים לשמחה

Moadim LeSimcha
Explorations Into
the Jewish Holidays

מועדים לשמחה

RABBI SHLOMO AVINER

Sifriyat Chava

URIM PUBLICATIONS

Jerusalem • New York

Moadim LeSimcha: Explorations Into the Jewish Holidays
by Rabbi Shlomo Aviner
edited by Liora Silberstein
Copyright © 2002 by Shlomo Aviner

The articles in this book have been translated from the two volumes of *Tal Chermon* by Rabbi Shlomo Aviner, as well as from articles on the festivals by the author.

All the articles have been translated from the Hebrew by **Bracha Slae**, with the exception of the following:

Y. Baumol: "Making Miracles Happen – Does God Need Our Help?"

R. Blumberg: *"Teshuva* and Joy"; *"Teshuva* and Acceptance of Guilt"; *"Teshuva* is Not Easy"; "Where was God During the Holocaust?" and "Was the Torah Forced Upon Us at Sinai?"

Rabbi Zeff: "The Days of Purim Will Never Be Nullified."

ISBN 965-7108-44-6

Urim Publications, P.O.Box 52287, Jerusalem 91521 Israel

Lambda Publishers Inc.
3709 13ᵗʰ Avenue Brooklyn, New York 11218 U.S.A.
Tel: 718-972-5449 Fax: 718-972-6307
Email: mh@ejudaica.com

www.UrimPublications.com

Designed by Raphaël Freeman
Typeset in Garamond by Jerusalem Typesetting

Contents

Rosh Hashana and Yom Kippur
The High Holy Days

Teshuva and Joy

QUESTION: Should we regard the sins that we commit as a trial sent by God? If one stumbles and sins, the feelings evoked are the opposite of joy: a sense of despair and failure. Is there a place for joy in serving God after falling into sin?

ANSWER: A person's reaction to sin is, in fact, a test in itself. Every sin comprises three parts: the sin itself, the emotional descent which follows the sin, and a new sin which may result from this. As we know, "one sin often leads to another."[1] After sinning, therefore, one must strengthen oneself and not fall into despair, but rather ascend higher than before. It is not enough to return to the situation in which one stood before the sin; one must utilize the energizing potential of the sin once it has occurred, do *teshuva* (repent) and elevate oneself.

Every sin should cause two opposing, yet complementary, feelings within the soul. On the one hand, one must be brokenhearted for transgressing the will of God. On the other hand, one must rejoice at the opportunity to do *teshuva*. The sorrow one feels after sinning should turn into gladness, for the very fact that one feels distraught at every point of darkness is a sign of purity in one's inner soul. If someone sins and does not feel the sting of regret, this should serve as a red flag that warns of great destruction within the soul, and then a thorough overhaul of one's moral character should begin.

The Torah was not given to people who never sin, but rather to people who sin and do *teshuva*: "There is no *tzaddik* on earth who only does good and does not sin."[2] Even a *tzaddik* sometimes stumbles. Only an evildoer

9

does not fall – because he or she is in a perpetual state of decline. There are no easy tricks or gimmicks for how to be victorious over the evil inclination. It is a long and arduous war; the one who will ultimately succeed is the one who is the most stubborn. "The *tzaddik* falls seven times and rises each time,"[3] but in the end will rise and will fall no more.

The constant grief resulting from sin – which eats away at one's spirit like a terminal illness – is also one of the evil inclination's cunning tactics. The evil inclination is an old king who is well versed in war, but we are already familiar with his strategy. When he finds a gentle and noble soul before him who has stumbled and transgressed, he does not say, "See how pleasant it was to sin; continue in this path." He knows that he will not find a listening ear. He therefore employs the opposite strategy hurling such accusations as: "You're base and despicable; you've already been excommunicated from the World to Come; you'll never manage to elevate yourself again." The anguished transgressor loses hope and falls deep into despair, wallowing in sin.

King Shlomo said, "Do not be too evil." Our Sages ask, "Is one allowed to be even a little evil?!" Rather, the meaning of, "Do not be too evil," can be compared to someone who has eaten garlic and the aroma has spread. Should he then eat more so that the aroma will spread further? Each person may stumble and sin at times; the essential thing is that one never despair of doing *teshuva* in the fear that there is no hope. Instead, he or she must overcome the sin and rise to the level of a *ba'al teshuva* – who stands in the place of a *tzaddik*.[4]

Teshuva as the Fundamental Basis of the Universe

I T SAYS IN THE TALMUD that *"teshuva* precedes the world."[5] This statement is not chronological, but causal. In other words, *teshuva* enables the world to exist and is the foundation of our lives. The world is dynamic, everything is in motion; there is constant activity as the world progresses in an unceasing upward process of self-perfection.

The world was purposely created in an imperfect state, so that it could be enhanced and perfected. This process of improvement is the essence of *teshuva*, which is not only the transformation of evil to good, but also the progression from good to better. There does not exist a person who is a *"tzaddik* in this world who only does good and never sins." Even in the absence of concrete sins, we are constantly required to elevate ourselves from one level to the next. Doing less than one is able is a sign of failure, and is a sin in itself.

Superficially, *teshuva* can be viewed as a negative process: you sinned, you do *teshuva*. Better yet, don't sin and you won't have to do *teshuva*. This is not the correct perspective. *Teshuva* is *a priori*, not *de facto*. It is a positive, dynamic, Divine drive for improvement, not merely a desirable action taken in order to reverse an undesirable one. Just as an infant has an unconscious drive for growth – just as every blade of grass has "an angel telling it to grow" – so, too, are there inner forces that drive mankind in general, and *Am Yisrael* in particular, to improve. Thus, the world is constantly changing, improving, and striving toward perfection.

Even when the world reaches its final, ideal state, it will still be dynamic.

The Sages tell us that "Torah scholars have no rest in this world nor in the World to Come, as it is written: 'They shall proceed from strength to strength.'"[6] There is always another world following the world which preceded it, *ad infinitum*. Tranquility comes not from rest, but from the unceasing progression from strength to strength. This is the true attainment of peace and joy.

Return to the original Divine plan for the world

The word *teshuva* means "return." To where do we return – for does not the word "return" imply a previous situation? The term *chozer beteshuva* is used for a person who was born irreligious, but who "returns" to religion. To what is he or she returning? The person is returning to the original, true nature of a human being who is created in the image of God. The Holy One created humans as decent, honorable beings, but they did not behave in an upright manner, and problems arose. As it says in *Kohelet*, "God created mankind to be upright but they have sought out many inventions."[7] In fact, the world itself was created in an ideal form, but it subsequently went awry. There is a disparity between the ideal world – representing the will of God – and the reality that ensued. The process of *teshuva* entails returning to the original Divine order.

In *Bereishit* we read, "And the Lord said: 'Let there be light.' And there was light." It does not say, "And it was so," as it does with the other creations. The implication is that a different kind of light than that originally envisioned by the Master of the World came into being. God had wanted to fill the world with the light of goodness, wisdom and truth. However, the world that evolved was unworthy of that original, Divinely conceived light, and it was therefore hidden away for the righteous in the World to Come.[8] The light which actually permeates the world is constantly developing over the generations, building up to perfection in the End of Days. A similar process happened on the third day: "And the Lord said, 'Let the earth bring forth… fruit trees yielding fruit after its kind.' And the earth brought forth…trees producing fruit."[9] The Divine plan was to produce trees in which the bark would have the same taste as the fruit, but in reality the earth brought forth fruit-bearing trees, in which only the fruit itself tasted like fruit.[10]

We see, then, that the world around us is not exactly in line with the

Divine plan. Our existence, too, is replete with pitfalls and shortcomings, but when we do *teshuva*, we are returning to the original Divine plan of the Master of the World.

Teshuva – repairing a broken and sinful world

A paradox is thus inherent in our world: It was created perfect and completely good, but in reality, it is now imperfect and disordered. Although the world is filled with flaws, it possesses an inherent ability to achieve perfection, accompanied by the certainty that this will ultimately occur. We may compare this to a person who wants to purchase a table. In the shop, he is given all kinds of wooden pieces, but he fails to understand. Is this a table? Yes, it is a "Do-It-Yourself" table. Our fragmented world is also destined to be "assembled." We know that all the necessary pieces are there and that they are meant to fit together perfectly. We can be certain that it is possible to build a perfect human being – and a perfect world – from these pieces. The process of "Do-It-Yourself," of achieving perfection, is what *teshuva* is all about.

The statement, "*Teshuva* precedes the world," implies that the world was purposely created in such a way that only the process of *teshuva* can elevate it to its true nature and destiny. Therefore, the problems and flaws that we see all around us need not cause despair, for God also created *teshuva* – the ability to rectify and elevate all that is imperfect. The Holy One created a world in which reality is flawed, with stumbling blocks in place and humanity destined to sin. He also created it with the potential to overcome all obstacles, and to be redeemed from its imperfections, through the power of *teshuva*. We are not responsible for the fact that the world was created with the possibility of sin, but neither are we exempted from the responsibility to remedy its ills, bringing it toward perfection.

There are three states in existence: The first state comprises mankind and the universe in their truest and most ideal form, as they were envisioned by the Divine. The second state is mankind and the universe as they actually exist, with all their imperfections and complications. The third state consists of the return to the first state. However, the third state is more exalted than the first, for the precise reason that it follows the second. The process of overcoming imperfections and inadequacies, and elevating the world to its ideal state by remedying its failures, is the concept of *teshuva*.

This begs the question: Why didn't God create the world in its perfect state from the very beginning? Why must the world undergo catastrophes in order to achieve perfection? We don't know the answer to this, but we do know that this must be the better way, for this is how God chose to make the world operate. Alternatively, we may understand that God did indeed create a world that is perfect, but in stages. To what may this be compared? To a man who brings some cloth to his tailor to sew him a suit. A few days later, he goes to see how the suit is coming along, and the tailor shows him many cut-up pieces of cloth. The man protests, "Not only have you failed to make me a suit, you have also ruined my cloth!" The tailor laughs and replies, "This is your suit. I'm still in the middle of making it." So, too, God is still in the process of creating a perfect world, and we are the vehicles through which He completes the job. It is a great honor for us to be His partners in creation.

Universal teshuva and personal teshuva

Usually, the concept of *teshuva* is thought of in relation to an individual who needs to correct a sin committed in his or her private life. R. Avraham Yitzchak Kook, however, taught that *teshuva* is a general spiritual phenomenon. Besides personal *teshuva*, there is also national *teshuva*, and even the *teshuva* of all existence: universal *teshuva*.[11]

The statement that *"teshuva* precedes the world" implies that *teshuva* existed even before mankind was created, when there were no sins or sinners. It is the essence and foundation of the universe. Therefore, an individual's *teshuva* forms part of the universal process of *teshuva*. As the Talmud teaches us, if one person repents, not only are his or her sins forgiven, but also those of the entire universe.[12]

Teshuva does not begin with the individual; rather, waves of *teshuva* cascade over all existence in a perpetual movement of growth and ascendance. The question for all of us is: Are we aware of this? Can we hear the echo of the universe? Do we desire to play an active part in this process? Do we wish to become contributing partners in the movement towards perfection, or do we not? Unfortunately, we may remain deaf to the call, believing that the universe is static and unchangeable; we thus remain in a frozen state of helplessness.

The universe is disordered; all of existence is fragmented and forlorn. But slowly, with resistance every step of the way, it is being uplifted. It is in the midst of a universal war. The universe calls out for perfection, roaring like a lioness in the throes of labor. We are told that, "Every day a *bat kol* (heavenly voice) from Mount Horev cries: 'Woe to my creatures who insult the Torah.'"[13] The voice of the universe cries out to mankind: Can't you hear? Can't you feel the pain? Aren't you ashamed?

Sometimes we do hear. We sense the voiceless *bat kol* inside us, and we realize that things cannot go on in this way. The very negativity of the current state of affairs empowers us, providing us with the motivation to correct and improve ourselves. We hear the echoes of the universal war and are filled with courage to join the struggle for perfection. Just like soldiers, when we find ourselves alone and isolated on the battlefield, we are less motivated to fight. But when we can fight side by side with our fellow-soldiers, and we hear the sounds of battle all around us, we, too, are filled with the will to fight. The echo causes us to be elevated, as well, for upon hearing it, we are filled with a desire to be a part of the upward trend of the world, and to help, not hinder, the process. These voices that we hear are known as "thoughts of *teshuva*." They do not originate inside us, but rather filter in from the world around us. We absorb the echo of the voice of the universe, which awakens thoughts of *teshuva* and the will to redeem our errors.

When an individual does *teshuva*, it should not emerge only from the perspective of his or her own personal spiritual shortcomings. This is egocentric and narrow-minded. Instead, a person should do collective *teshuva* as part of *Am Yisrael* and as part of the universe. No man is an island. If we were, it would be easy, in this lonely, sorry state, to fall into despair. However, once we are aware that we are not alone, we assume responsibility for the whole universe. When we are attuned to the pain of the universe, we feel impelled to relieve it. Thus, ideally, the desire for perfection stems not from egoism, but from a sense of responsibility for, and partnership with, the whole universe.

This does not mean that a person should focus on correcting the faults of others. It goes without saying that one should correct one's own shortcomings before rebuking others for theirs. Nevertheless, personal *teshuva* stems from awareness of the universal. A true desire for universal perfection expresses itself, first and foremost, in a desire to uplift that one small part of existence that is oneself – one's own personal life. Thus, individual *teshuva* is an extension of the concept of the universal.

General terms such as *"Klal Yisrael"* and "universal existence" are sometimes misunderstood, as if these concepts downgrade the worth and contribution of the individual. Some say that it is more important for a person to navigate through the complex, tricky maze of life than to concentrate on universal issues. Of course, there is a need for self-inspection, but it should take place within the context of communal awareness. Identification as part of a group does not nullify one's personal needs, but rather uplifts them.

The Divine command, "Let there be light," paves the way for the universe in wisdom, justice, sanctity and social values, and impels the world to follow a perpetual path of *teshuva*. Similarly, the individual must spend his or her whole life in *teshuva*, progressing from bad to good, and from small to great – always advancing, never standing still.

This is the partnership forged between mankind and God. The Holy One created *teshuva* as the fundamental basis of the universe, and consequently, the world is permeated with a drive for this elevated state. We hear, in the depths of our souls, the voice of God calling to us; we are constantly flooded with thoughts of *teshuva*. Even the wicked are filled with regret, though they may sublimate these feelings. The question is what we choose to do with all these thoughts of *teshuva*, for we have free will. On the one hand, we may reject these thoughts for fear of taking responsibility, or because of the despair, distress and bitterness which we experience as a result of our condition. On the other hand, we may choose to acknowledge these thoughts – despite the great difficulty involved – and be uplifted by them, thus elevating the world.

The inevitability of teshuva vs. free will

The Torah promises that *Am Yisrael* will ultimately do *teshuva*, as it is written, "And you shall return to the Lord your God."[14] Accordingly, we might think that we can relax our great efforts to improve our ways. After all, we know that our *teshuva* is guaranteed – God has promised us that we will return, and we have faith in Him. This is all very well and good, but the Torah does not disclose how and when this will happen. We have no way of knowing how much time it will take, or how much suffering we will have to undergo, until that point. It depends upon us. God's Divine promise to us does not preclude our own efforts. Rather, it is our human achievement that leads to its realization. The very fact that such a promise exists impels us to action, for we know that our efforts will not be in vain.

A similar misconception applies to the Divine pledge of inheriting *Eretz Yisrael*. There are those who claim that since God has promised the Holy Land to our forefathers, we should wait in the Diaspora for Him to keep His promise. We must have faith in God, they say, and that means not taking the initiative to conquer and settle *Eretz Yisrael* ourselves. Doing so would be a sign of rebellion against God and would indicate an implicit lack of faith in the Divine promise.

However, in the very same passage of the Torah, in which God promises to give us *Eretz Yisrael*, He also commands us: "Come and inherit the Land."[15] That task is our responsibility. Precisely because God has sworn to give us the Land, He commands us to inherit it. Had He not sworn that it would be ours, there would be no point in fighting for it. But once the promise is made, we are sure that our efforts will be successful.

So it is regarding *teshuva*: God has promised that we will do *teshuva*. This means that He is telling us that *teshuva* is possible, that it is the foundation of the world, and that the world will eventually reach its ultimate goal. However, this will only come to fruition through our efforts. The world is a "Do-It-Yourself" project for which we have been given the necessary tools to complete the job.

Equipped with this knowledge, we are motivated to meet our challenges, confident that our efforts will not be in vain. We are sure that we shall ultimately succeed, even if we stumble once, twice, or three times. We shall continue to try, over and over again, because that is the essence of reality and of history. The Divine light impels us forward ceaselessly. We have been blessed with both physical and spiritual capabilities for growth. This is the power of *teshuva*, the power that builds the universe and imbues it with meaning.

Teshuva and Acceptance of Guilt

R*AMBAM* STATES: "Since everyone has free will, one should strive to repent, to confess one's sins verbally and to shake them off."[16] It is quite puzzling that our great master *Rambam* did not write explicitly in *Hilchot Teshuva* that there is a *mitzva* to repent, but only that *when* we repent, we must verbally confess our sins.

Teshuva is not a finite act such as Shabbat or *Kashrut*; putting on *tefillin* or wearing *tzitzit*; or helping one's fellow. Rather, it is a process that encompasses one's whole life. The Sages said, "Repent one day before you die,"[17] and since no one knows when that will be, one must do *teshuva* every day.

Neither is *teshuva* merely one aspect of life. Rather, it is our *raison d'être*. The Sages coined a priceless phrase: "*ba'al teshuva*." Literally, this means "master of *teshuva*," and is similar to the expression "*ba'al lashon hara*" – literally, "master of gossip." Clarifying the different levels of gossip, as enumerated at the end of *Rambam's Hilchot De'ot*, will help us to understand what a master of *teshuva* is:

1 *Rechilut*, or talebearing. The sin of *rechilut* is telling stories about someone in such a way as to create resentment and strife. This is a severe sin. Yet there is another act even more severe:

2 *Lashon Hara*, or evil gossip. This means relating *negative* things about one's fellow. This causes harm and creates fear, even if the gossip is true. Still worse is:

3 *Motzi Shem Ra*. This is when one speaks negatively about someone using false information. Yet what follows is worst of all:

4 *Ba'al Lashon Hara*. This refers to the chronic gossip. Even if someone

only gossips once, or on very rare occasions, that is severe. Yet the *ba'al lashon hara* is one who uses every opportunity to speak ill of others.

There may well be exceptional cases in which speaking negatively about a person is permissible, in much the same way that one may drive on Shabbat in order to bring a dangerously ill person to the hospital. Yet just as Shabbat is not open to laxity and abuse, neither is speech. In the same way that the *ba'al lashon hara* chronically speaks evil gossip, so is the *ba'al teshuva*, throughout his or her life, occupied with repentance. He or she faces constant tension and is involved in a ceaseless struggle to grow in goodness.

Therefore, it is not quite appropriate to say that there is a *mitzva* to repent. Rather, *teshuva* represents the whole content of our lives. How do we know that this is what *Rambam* means? In order to answer this, we need to analyze his choice of words: "Since everyone has free will, one should strive to repent, to confess one's sins verbally and to shake them off."

Why does it say, "one should *strive*"? Are we not, in fact, obligated? Rather, there are infinite levels of *teshuva*. That is why *Rambam* links *teshuva* to free will. Mankind has free will: we are able to control our thoughts, speech and actions. Therefore, one must *strive* toward *teshuva* and continuously invest one's utmost effort, never remaining in the same place, but always ascending ever higher.

Verbal confession

In the beginning of *Rambam's Hilchot Teshuva*, we read: "If a person has transgressed any *mitzva* in the Torah…when he does *teshuva* and repents from his sin, he is obligated to verbally confess his sins before God."[18] Why is a verbal confession so important?

The reason that verbal confession is essential to the *teshuva* process is that it constitutes acceptance of responsibility. All people sin; we are not angels. The question is how we deal with our sins. Do we admit that we have sinned and accept responsibility, or do we blame others for our shortcomings? We must not argue that what we did was not a sin or that it was not our fault, but rather the fault of our spouses, parents, neighbors, friends, the government, the army, etc.

People have a tendency to blame others. Even Adam claimed in his own defense that he ate the forbidden fruit because of his wife.[19] How ungrateful! God had given him a marvelous gift and he blamed Chava for his own failings. It is human nature to pretend to ourselves that someone else is guilty of our sins. R. Avraham Yitzchak Kook wrote that most people prefer to live in a fantasy world rather than view life rationally. Instead of seeing the truth as it is, they see it as they would like it to be, viewing reality through the prism of the imagination. How many tragedies have occurred because we were deceived by our desires! For example, before World War II, governments imagined that if territorial concessions were made to Hitler – may his name be blotted out – there would be peace. In the same way, most people in their personal lives are captives of their imaginations, unable to admit the truth to themselves.

When someone articulates the words, "I have sinned," it is a victory of clear, truthful reason over misleading fantasies. That is not to say that there is no place for the imagination. The fact that we possess this power tells us that the Master of the Universe intends for us to use it. Imagination can lead to great things; one of the prerequisites for prophecy is a pure, pristine imagination. When the Zionist movement was stalled, Dr. Theodor Herzl wrote a book, *Altneuland* (New-Old Land), a novel about an idealized country inhabited by an imaginary tribe. Today, thank God, the reality of Zionism surpasses his dreams.

The important point is that we have to beware of our imagination, for it is slippery and unreliable. It hovers on the border between good and evil. It can bring us renewal and creativity, or it can delude us. Obviously, the employment of logic can lead to error as well, but when one is in tune with one's rational self, the goal is to see the truth.

Why, then, do people allow themselves to suffer from illusions? They find that it is unpleasant to admit mistakes, that it is depressing, breaks the spirit and causes despair. They believe that denial of their shortcomings will empower them, whereas admitting to themselves, to God and to other people that they have acted improperly will destroy their self-image. They therefore prefer to imagine that they are innocent and that it is others who are the sinners.

This is a grievous error indeed! If we imagine that we are innocent and pure, and that all of our failings are due to others, then we are truly lost, for we have no chance of self-improvement. That is a true cause of despair. If, however, one says, "I am guilty, it is I who sinned," that is certainly a cause of sadness, but it is a source of happiness as well, for we can then actively improve our condition. R. Nachman of Breslov said, "If you believe that it is possible to make mistakes, then you can believe that it is also possible to make amends." Such a belief fills one with great joy.

Not only do verbal confession and *teshuva* reflect an acceptance of responsibility on the part of the one who sinned, but they are necessary for another reason. A verbal confession requires a person to think clearly and to dare to express his or her feelings. Thoughts can be hazy and unfocused, as well as less binding. Speech, on the other hand, is full of clarity and strength.

Verbal confession in the Tanach

In the *Tanach*, we read of two kings of Israel who sinned; one confessed and one didn't. When King Shaul sinned by not killing Amalek, the prophet Shmuel chastised him. How did Shaul respond? He blamed the people for his sins![20] It was certainly true that the people had a part to play in his sin, as *Netziv* points out, and that the king had to contend with his subjects' foolish demands. Still, this is not a fitting response from a real leader.

In contrast, after King David's serious sin involving Batsheva, and the prophet Natan's subsequent rebuke, David responded in a manner that is exceedingly rare in our world: he said, "I have sinned!"[21] That reply took enormous courage and strength. The Sages say that David's sin provided a valuable lesson for *Am Yisrael* and for mankind, so we could hear a great man – a king, no less – declare, "I have erred." The fact that David admitted his mistake did not lessen his greatness. After all, we are human, and we make mistakes.

We human beings err, repent and move forward in such a way that our entire lives are spent doing *teshuva*. In order for this cycle to stay in motion, we must rise above our imaginations. As stated above, our powers of reason can err sometimes as well. Yet that problem has a solution: friends can help us become aware of our mistakes. We must be prepared to accept the critique of our friends, even or especially when they tell us things that we don't like to hear.

God said regarding Chava, "I will make [for Adam] a helper (*ezer*) opposite him (*kenegdo*)."[22] The Sages explain, "If he merits it, she will be a helper. Otherwise, she will oppose him."[23] Ultimately, however, both the words *ezer* and *kenegdo* appear in the same verse, implying that both opposition and support can coexist in a relationship. *Netziv* further adds that the very way that a man's wife helps him is by her standing in opposition to him. If she merely nods her head and agrees with everything her husband says, he will never encounter the dynamic exchange of ideas which might refine his views and lead to self-improvement.

Teshuva Is Not Easy

QUESTION: Even as I confess my sins, I realize that I am most likely going to continue to fail in some of these areas. How can I stand before the Master of the Universe and express contrition and real resolve regarding the future?

ANSWER: What you describe is, in fact, true contrition, albeit not strong enough to withstand the probable onslaught of the evil inclination. It is real *teshuva*, although it is not complete *teshuva*, and it should not be made light of.

Teshuva is something so enormous, so remarkable – penetrating so much of the spiritual universe – that even a tiny morsel of *teshuva* is considered to be something great, and its light permeates the soul, giving one the strength to ascend to ever higher levels of greatness.

Just as Redemption occurs gradually, so does *teshuva* – step by step, effort after effort, until all the little efforts add up to a great sum. Fortunate is one who repents fully all at once; fortunate is one who is transformed into another person overnight. This was the case with R. Elazar ben Dordia, who fell into the depths of sin, and at a certain point came to the realization of how far he had fallen. He broke out in tears and cried out, "I am the only one who can save myself!" As his soul flew up to Heaven, a heavenly voice went forth and proclaimed: "R. Elazar ben Dordia is invited to the World to Come." R. Yehuda HaNassi wept and said, "There are those who acquire their world after many years of effort, and there are those who acquire it in a single moment."[24]

Most of us are incapable of sudden *teshuva*, of the spiritual lightning that, in a moment, banishes all sin. But we are capable of gradual *teshuva*, of slowly improving ourselves, as we ascend higher and higher, of laboriously traversing the paths of righteousness, of painstakingly refining our character traits and deeds – until we reach the high spiritual level of *tahara*, or purity.[25]

Even when a person merely thinks about *teshuva*, wishes to repent and decides to repent, but is not yet capable of carrying it out, this in itself already causes a great light to shine in his or her soul. Imagine a country that is corrupt, yet whose spiritual figures protest forcefully against the corruption. Compare this to another morally bankrupt country, one whose leaders bow their heads before wickedness. This country is as different from the first as night is from day. While the first country has hope for a better future, the second has no chance for improvement. In the same way, when we confess, we are protesting against the wickedness within our souls. By doing so, we bring ourselves into the presence of God's light.

Our master, R. Avraham Yitzchak Kook, writes: "A person is obligated to confess his sins....When he experiences daily the purity of prayer and confession – while never forgetting to analyze his own deeds – he is shaking off his own wickedness, little by little, before that wickedness can deceive him so greatly that he is unable to lift his head."[26]

Therefore, on the one hand, *teshuva* is the easiest *mitzva* there is, because even the very act of thinking penitent thoughts constitutes *teshuva*. On the other hand, it is the most difficult *mitzva*, because *teshuva* only comes after great toil.[27] Therefore, one shouldn't let one's spirit sink when one sees oneself rise and fall, as it says in *Mishlei*, "The *tzaddik* falls seven times and rises each time."[28] Ultimately, he will stop falling. In contrast, the evildoer lies fallen in despair. Even the righteous sometimes fall in battle, yet what is even worse than that is to fall without ever having gone to war.

Therefore, we must stand courageously in the presence of God's light, strengthening our resolve to repent. Then our *teshuva* is guaranteed, for the Master of the Universe will not abandon us, but will help us to achieve holiness.

The Significance of the *Shofar*

THE *SHOFAR* SIGNALS both the birth and the future of *Am Yisrael*. In the *mussaf* prayer on Rosh Hashana, we recall the giving of the Torah: "You revealed Yourself to Your holy people in the cloud of Your glory in order to speak to them, You revealed Yourself to them in thunder and lightning, and You appeared to them through the sound of the *shofar*."[29] Yeshayahu also tells us that in the final Redemption, "It shall be that on that day, a great *shofar* will be blown, and those who were lost in the land of Ashur will come, as well as those who were cast aside in the land of Egypt, and they shall bow down before God on the holy mountain, in Jerusalem."[30]

The Creator revealed His Divine will through the *shofar* at *Matan Torah*. The ultimate purpose of the events at Sinai is the future revelation of God's light throughout the world at the final Redemption: "A great *shofar* will be blown...and they shall bow down before God on the holy mountain, in Jerusalem."

According to *Chassidut*, the passage from *Yeshayahu* mentions two types of Jews: those "lost" (*ha'ovdim*) in Ashur and those "cast aside" (*hanidachim*) in Egypt. The land of Ashur is the land of ecstasy and bliss.[31] Some people get "lost" in all the bliss, as the Torah teaches: "And Yeshurun [*Am Yisrael*] became fat and he kicked."[32] Too much physical and material delight can cause *Am Yisrael* to extinguish the sparks of divinity in their souls; these sparks drown in the flood of wordly pleasures and foreign influences to which they are constantly exposed.

Another group of people is "cast aside" in Egypt, where suffering causes them to abandon God: "And they did not listen to Moshe on account of distress and hard work."[33] Their nobleness of spirit was eroded by their many trials and hardships. The great *shofar* of Redemption will awaken those who have fallen into the clutches of Ashur and those who have been swallowed up by Egypt. *Rambam* teaches: "Although the blowing of the *shofar* on Rosh Hashana is a *mitzva* for which no reason is stated, it is as if the *shofar* were suggesting, 'Arise from your sleep, you who slumber. Repent with contrition. Remember your Creator. Peer into your soul and improve your ways and your deeds.'"[34]

This is also the message of R. Amnon, the holy author of the *"Unetaneh tokef"* prayer in *mussaf* of Rosh Hashana: "A great *shofar* blast shall sound, and a still, small voice will be heard." If a great *shofar* is blown, how can the sound be still and small? The answer is that on that awesome day, one hears an inner voice – the voice of the soul, the Divine speaking from within. The *shofar* blast is the catalyst which frees our soul from its fetters and grants us the power to hear: "And a still, small voice will be heard."

The Forces of Evil

In the beginning of *parashat Acharei Mot*, we find the Yom Kippur service, including the laws of the *Se'ir L'Azazel* – the goat which was first dedicated as a sacrifice and then sent out to the wilderness, to *Azazel*, to die, instead of being offered up in the *Beit HaMikdash*. This seems very strange – almost, God forbid, similar to the idolatrous practices of bribing and placating the forces of evil.

The forces of evil are neither independent nor controlled by any power except God's alone. Satan himself is one of God's fleet of angels, sent to carry out His will in this world, as we read in *Iyov*. Mankind is not responsible for the existence of evil in this world. When God created this imperfect world, He provided it with the potential for sin and iniquity, just as when He created light, He allowed for the possibility of darkness.

Mankind, however, is duty-bound to do everything in its power to perfect the world by correcting its wrongs and returning to God. In this way, mankind "helps" the Creator. The two goats brought as sacrifices on Yom Kippur symbolize this partnership. One goat is offered to God, to atone for our failure to live up to this responsibility – this is the sin-offering of *teshuva*. The other goat is the *Se'ir L'Azazel*, which seemingly comes to atone for God Himself, the Creator of evil. Our sins are not merely the result of our misdeeds; they stem from the potential for evil inherent in this world, as symbolized by the desert – the home of emptiness and desolation, where the *Se'ir* is doomed to die.

Once we understand that evil is no more than a tool of the Creator, which He uses according to His will alone, we learn to accept, and even respect, its existence. Although evil is tainted and destructive, and it is incumbent upon us to distance ourselves from it, it is important to recognize that it was only created to fulfill the will of God. Evil is only able to exist because of this spark of holiness, i.e., the role it plays in perfecting the world. Therefore, it is not to be scorned.[35]

We must distinguish between absolute truth and the way we learn, in practice, to lead our lives. In absolute terms, there is no real evil. All defects are merely stages in the process of achieving perfection. However, from our limited perception, evil does exist in this world, and it is our responsibility to educate ourselves and others to recognize and fight against it. Every now and then, we must also recall that evil has no inherent value, but merely serves to contrast with good and to enhance its value. Therefore, once a year on Yom Kippur, on the day of sanctification and purification, we send out the *Se'ir L'Azazel*. In this way, we are affirming that when all is said and done, the forces of evil were created to serve God and to ultimately lead to good.

Erev Yom Kippur: Forgiving One Another

On YOM KIPPUR we generally devote much energy to our relationship with God: to *teshuva* and to prayer. However, we all know that even on Yom Kippur, God does not forgive sins committed against others unless the wronged person has already pardoned us. Naturally, there is no one who has not hurt his or her fellow in some way during the year, whether intentionally or unintentionally. Everyone has some trace of negative feeling toward someone else.

To remedy these feelings of antipathy, *Arizal* added a prayer to the nightly recital of the *Kriyat Shema*. We proclaim: "I forgive everyone who has angered me, provoked me, or sinned against me, whether physically, monetarily, emotionally, or in any other way, whether accidentally or purposefully, whether he was aware or unaware." If all Jews would recite this, we could go to sleep at night with a clear conscience. The problem is that we don't all do so. And even if we do, we don't always mean it.

For this reason, there is an additional prayer, the *Tefilla Zaka*, recited on the eve of Yom Kippur, in which we resolve to forgive all those who have harmed us. Of course, not everyone says this prayer either. Therefore, the only solution is that every one of us, without exception, must forgive everyone else. All of *Am Yisrael* must enter into a contract with one another: that we will forgive if everyone else forgives. This enables God to forgive us, for one who forgives and overlooks the sins of others is treated likewise by God.

Of course, to effect true forgiveness, we must absolve others wholeheartedly. There are three lines of thought which may help us to achieve this goal:

1 We must realize that we ourselves also sin, and are very often guilty of the same type of wrongdoing for which we blame others. We tend to project our shortcomings onto others and to see our own faults reflected in them. To counteract this, we must bear in mind that other people are as humanly fallible as we are.

2 We must recognize that the other person is fundamentally a decent human being. He or she may have faults, but these should not be exaggerated. There are certain people who may arouse in us feelings of hostility, but we must keep things in proportion, and train ourselves to look at others positively, "with a good eye."[36]

3 We must accept upon ourselves, for the future, not to hate anyone – neither at work, in the community, nor in the family. This does not mean that we should never rebuke anyone, but it must be done gently and with love, so that it will ultimately achieve its goal.

Sukkot

A Celebration of Life

Our sages have noted that the *mitzva* of *sukka* is unique in that it is performed with the whole body. One walks into the *mitzva* of *sukka*, fully clothed, down to the mud on one's boots. In this way, the *mitzva* of *sukka* is similar to the *mitzva* of building *Eretz Yisrael*. There is even a source for this parallel in *Tehillim*: "And His *sukka* was in Shalem, and His dwelling place in Zion";[1] *sukka* is equated with Zion. The Vilna Gaon notes another similarity: Just as one is commanded to construct one's own *sukka* ("*ta'aseh ve'lo min ha'asui*"), so is one commanded to be personally involved in the *mitzva* of building *Eretz Yisrael*. These are acts which are blessed by God.

Moreover, one can even perform the *mitzva* of *sukka* while asleep. *Halacha* considers it more important to sleep in a *sukka* than to eat in it. This indicates that there are *mitzvot* which, by their very nature, a Jew performs unconsciously – a sign of the unique quality of the Jewish soul. (Likewise, the *mitzva* of living in *Eretz Yisrael* is also fulfilled while asleep.)

On Sukkot, we demonstrate that we are in love with life in this world; with our whole being, we immerse ourselves in the *mitzva*. We fulfill the *mitzva* with our bodies, even when our intellect and consciousness are asleep. In contrast, on Yom Kippur, we minimize our ties with the physical world, in imitation of the angels. As soon as the fast of Yom Kippur ends, we begin to build our *sukkot*,[2] emphasizing the connection between these two seemingly opposite *mitzvot*, which together demonstrate the distinctive nature of the Jewish soul. Sukkot does not signify a spiritual decline from Yom Kippur. On the contrary, the "other-worldly" sanctity of Yom Kippur is absorbed in the "this-worldly," tangible *mitzva* of *sukka*.

Our Sages debated which type of *shofar* is preferable – straight or bent – and finally ruled that a *shofar* should be bent. The reason for this is that during the High Holidays, we emphasize the spiritual, and the material must bow down before it. However, after this period of spiritual purification, we return to the physical, material world with the *lulav* in our hands. A kosher *lulav*, in contrast to the *shofar*, has to be straight. If it is bent or bowed, it is disqualified, for the *lulav* must stand upright in its sacredness.

What Does Sukkot Commemorate?

THE TALMUD DISCUSSES what it is that we commemorate on Sukkot. R. Eliezer claims that the huts in which we dwell on Sukkot represent the actual huts in which *Am Yisrael* dwelt in the desert. R. Akiva maintains that the huts symbolize the Clouds of Glory which hovered over *Am Yisrael* in the desert.[3]

Huts in the desert

The forty years that *Am Yisrael* spent in the desert after leaving Egypt were a difficult test indeed. The men, women and children were threatened by snakes and scorpions, and had to cope with insufficient water,[4] unbearable heat during the day and biting frost at night.[5] Meanwhile, they hungered for real bread as opposed to *manna*.[6] These forty years of trials were God's way of educating *Am Yisrael* to appreciate the good and overcome the bad, to be satisfied with their lot, and to view life with a balanced perspective. Commemorating that period of challenge and growth equips us with the ability to come to terms with the positive and the negative that we experience.

Rambam in *Guide to the Perplexed* discusses the question of human suffering and divides it into three categories:

1 *Troubles that are caused by nature, e.g., natural disasters and various illnesses.* These affect a relatively small number of people. For the most part, people are healthy and do not become seriously ill or encounter natural disasters.

2 *Troubles that people cause one another, e.g., war, murder and other criminal acts.* In the two World Wars, close to 100 million people were killed.

Even here, one can say that the majority of people in the world are not affected in such a way.

3 *Troubles that one brings upon oneself.* These are the trials that affect the majority of people. This category includes physical pain that is caused by unhealthy eating habits or an indulgent lifestyle. Also included is emotional distress that is caused by unfulfilled expectations. We convince ourselves that we need a particular thing and that we can't live without it. When this happens, we feel acutely miserable, which leads us to challenge God with such theological questions as: "Why did you do this to me? Why is there so much suffering in the world?"

From this perspective, we can see that most of the suffering we feel is unnecessary. A person experiences much pain because of imagined desires and distorted expectations of life. The essential ingredients that one needs for daily life can generally be found within reach: air to breathe is free; water to drink is very inexpensive; food sufficient to sustain life is easily attained. The more vital the need, the greater its accessibility and readiness for consumption. The less critical the need, the less accessible and more expensive that item becomes.[7]

The forty years of hardship in the desert were part of God's plan to educate His nation. From our point of view, those forty years were a punishment for the Sin of the Spies; had we not sinned, we would have entered *Eretz Yisrael* immediately. However, what seems to us to be "after the fact" – an unexpected result of an undesirable choice – is "before the fact" to God. *Rambam* concludes that God's plan – causing us to stay so long in the hostile desert – was designed to teach us to appreciate the good in life and to be grateful for what we have been given.[8]

The lesson of courage

Our arduous life in the desert also trained us to be courageous. From a nation of weak, fearful slaves, we emerged a nation of fighters. When *Am Yisrael* saw the Egyptians pursuing them after leaving Egypt, they panicked and cried to Moshe, "Are there not enough graves in Egypt that you have to take us to the desert to die?! Why did you take us out of Egypt?"[9] The commentator, Ibn Ezra, asks the following question: "The Israelites numbered 600,000 armed soldiers. Why didn't they defend themselves against the Egyptians?" He explains that a slave is used to following his master's orders and lacks the courage to oppose him. The entire generation was incapable of standing up to the Canaanites. They therefore all had to die in the desert.

Difficult trials strengthen character, as opposed to "the good life" which, in excess, spoils people and weakens their ability to cope. The suffering in the desert was for our own good, as the verse says, "In order to try you and to test you, to benefit you at the end."[10] These tests prepared us and nurtured within us the strength of character that enabled us to fight during the conquering of *Eretz Yisrael* and during the other struggles that have been our lot over the years.

One could argue: We, the descendants of that generation, weren't in the desert and weren't tested with those difficulties. What relevance and benefit do their challenges have for us today? Just as a person can go through a powerful experience that has a great impact upon him or her, and will remain indelibly imprinted memory on a personal level, so, too, are there experiences that are forever engraved in our national psyche, so that subsequent generations and individuals still perceive them and feel their influence.

Clouds of Glory

The Divine Clouds of Glory surrounded and guided us through all the years we spent in the desert, as it says, "According to God's word they encamped, and according to God's word they traveled."[11] All our comings and goings were mandated by the Clouds of Glory. But were they really necessary? Isn't the whole world a witness to the Creator?[12]

It is true that all of creation proclaims God's glory,[13] but there are varying degrees in the revelation of God's grandeur in creation. Mankind, created in God's image, manifests a more refined level of God's glory than does the rest of creation, but the pinnacle of God's revelation in the world is through *Am Yisrael*. God's presence was revealed through us in the desert, hovering over us in all our nomadic wanderings. He did not abandon us to drift in the desert; rather, the traveling was part and parcel of Divine providence, as it says, "According to God's word they encamped, and according to God's word they traveled." The Clouds of Glory were the means by which God led us, watched over us and protected us. This is so despite all our sins during those forty years in the desert: the Golden Calf, the Sin of the Spies, the complaining, the promiscuity with the daughters of Moab, and so on. We have to know that notwithstanding our transgressions, God is always with us, as it says, "Who dwells with them amidst their impurity."[14]

Whether we realize it or not, Divine providence continually guides us and watches over us. Just as the Clouds of Glory were manifest yet also hazy, unclear, hidden and incomprehensible,[15] so is it hard for us today to discern the hand of God in everything that happens. There is much that we don't understand. The Torah itself was given in fog.[16] Just as the Torah contains some passages that we understand and others that are shrouded in mist, so, too, at times it is clear that God's hand is guiding our history, and at other times it is not. At times, the Divine handwriting is clear upon the wall; at others, it is hazy and illegible.[17] Who can fathom the Holocaust? Even with all the books, articles and explanations proffered, we are incapable of comprehending the facts, let alone the reasons behind it.

On the one hand we see in our days Divine guidance clearly revealed in the return to Zion, the building up of the Land, the establishment of the State and the miraculous military victories over our foes. But on the other hand, we are faced with threats from our enemies without, and even deep internal strife within. Many Jews are estranged from a life of Torah and *mitzvot*, and we often wonder if this is what we have prayed for throughout the generations. We need not worry; even these situations are part of God's carefully determined plan. Though the secrets of Divine providence are hard to grasp, we are not exempt from making an effort to perceive God's hand in the world. Ultimately, we must realize that the Clouds of Glory are always surrounding us, even in times of sin and suffering, whether we clearly see the hand of God or not.

In summary, the reason R. Elazar gives for the *mitzva* of *sukka* – that it commemorates the actual booths in which we lived in the desert – with all the lessons we learn from that, is a practical, human explanation. The reason R. Akiva gives for this *mitzva*, that it commemorates the Clouds of Glory (i.e., God's guidance at all times), is a spiritual explanation. There is no contradiction between the two. One can explain a phenomenon on two levels, either according to obvious, logical causes or according to God's hand that is working from afar. Divine providence acts in our history in a tangible direct way,[18] just as the Clouds of Glory are revealed when we sit in actual booths.

A time to rejoice

The holiday of Sukkot is also known as a time of rejoicing and happiness. Our forty years in the desert taught us to be happy with our portion in life and to overcome difficulty. We learned how to put into perspective the challenges, the difficulties, and the suffering in our lives, and how to accept our lot without being weakened or broken by it. We are capable of withstanding the test: every year we leave the comfort and security of our homes to live in huts for a week – with no complaint. We realize that God's Clouds of Glory envelop us and that the Master of the World is always with us, and this knowledge keeps us from becoming disheartened and pessimistic. Our forty difficult years of living in huts in the desert strengthened us. With this historic memory indelibly engraved in our national psyche, no difficulty can deter us. We are confident that only good will come from the challenges we face. We are happy and optimistic.

Today, too, our faith in God and confidence in His beneficial Providence colors our outlook on life. We have seen *Am Yisrael* reborn in our lifetime. Clearly, we have economic, political, ethical, and spiritual problems – but these are only fragments of a bigger picture. We must look at the course of history over the past century. Our rebirth is a continuous process. It began over a century ago, and may take many more centuries, but one thing is certain: it is the process of the Redemption of *Am Yisrael*.

It is an important principle in education that one cannot attempt to instill every value at once, for this would create confusion. Rather, we have to stick to priorities, to the most important values and beliefs, and constantly strengthen them. In our generation, the most central spiritual value is belief in the Redemption in our day. Our very belief in God rests upon our belief in the Redemption, for belief in God means that we trust that God is in charge of everything that happens in history. The belief that the history unfolding before our eyes today is a revelation of God's Will reinforces our faith in God and our acceptance of His sovereignty over all events, past, present and future. In other words, the key to strengthening all of *Am Yisrael*'s faith in God is to educate towards faith in the Divine providence which guides us today.

The *Mitzva* of Serving God with Joy

THE AIM OF THE TORAH is not to prevent us from living and enjoying our lives to the fullest. On the contrary, the Torah emphasizes, "And you, who cling to the Lord your God, you are all alive here today."[19] It is "here," living in this world, that we cling to God. The verse speaks to "all" of us, not just to the very righteous. And it refers to "today," not to the End of Days.

Failure to rejoice in the service of God is cause for punishment, as it is written, "Since you did not serve the Lord your God with joy and a full heart when you had everything, you shall [be punished and] serve your enemy."[20] True, you did serve God, but you brought exile upon yourselves because of your lack of joy in that service. *Rambam*, in his discussion of the *mitzva* of joy on Sukkot, teaches us the following general principle regarding the service of God:

The happiness with which one performs *mitzvot*, and the love one feels for the One who commanded us to do them, is in itself a vital service of God. Anyone who does not allow himself to rejoice deserves to be punished, as it is written, "Since you did not serve the Lord your God with joy and a full heart."[21]

It is not only the *mitzva* which is important, but also the manner in which one carries it out. One should, ideally, take pleasure in the fulfillment of *mitzvot*. There once was a convert who was asked by the Sages why he wanted to become Jewish. He answered: "The Jewish religion requires not only the body to be involved in fulfilling *mitzvot*, but also the heart and the soul. That is what makes it such a noble faith." We are not asked to fulfill the *mitzvot* grudgingly, feeling coerced and obligated. Rather, God wants us to rejoice in our service of Him, to feel fulfilled while carrying out His *mitzvot*.

Admittedly, though, it is no small feat to mobilize our intellectual, emotional and spiritual faculties to a complete identification with Torah and *mitzvot*.

Is service of God a joy or an obligation?

The principle that service of God needs to be performed with joy needs further clarification. Is the Jewish ideal to be happy and to enjoy life, or is it to fulfill our obligations and do what is required of us? The Greek philosopher Epicure turned the pursuit of pleasure into an ideal. It is true that he advocated enjoying life in a refined, measured manner – so as not to cause suffering to anyone – but his goal was simply to maximize pleasure. An Epicorus, or disciple of Epicure, is the term used by the Sages to describe a Jew whose philosophy of life contradicts Judaism. The Jewish ideal is not to pursue pleasure, but rather to do what is good in God's eyes, even when this doesn't make us happy – and even saddens us. Similarly, we reject the temptation to sin, no matter how pleasurable it may seem.

This sharpens the question as to what the Torah means by wanting us to serve God with joy. On the contrary, it seems that our service of God should be based solely upon our desire to discharge our obligations. On the face of it, one who derives pleasure from performing the *mitzvot* is doing so for personal fulfillment and not for the sake of Heaven. Service of God, then, becomes merely a means of self-gratification.

Let us look to interpersonal relationships in order to illuminate the principle of fulfilling the *mitzvot* with joy. A husband says to his wife: "Am I not a good husband? I do all the shopping, help you in the house, and fulfill all my marital obligations. True, I don't love you and I feel depressed living in this house with you, but I overcome my antipathy to you and I treat you well – because that's what my *mussar* books tell me to do!" What a *tzaddik*! How would you feel if you were his wife? What difference does it make that he treats her nicely if his heart is elsewhere? Just as it is obvious that such an attitude in a husband to his wife, or in one friend to another, is degrading and of no value, so it is between us and God. Carrying out *mitzvot* without investing one's heart and soul is akin to telling God: "Your *mitzvot* don't interest me. They are a burden and I hate them. I'd rather do other things, but I have no choice; that is why I observe *mitzvot*. I love to eat nonkosher food and behave permissively, but I abstain. I hate my wife and other people, but I am commanded to treat them well, so I do. I am a disciplined soldier, a 'Cossack' in the service of God."

Is this the ideal approach? Absolutely not! There is something fundamentally lacking in one's service of God if it is joyless. Granted, it is not always easy to serve God happily – sometimes it is harder than the *mitzva* itself – but real service of God should not just be an external act of discharging one's obligations, carried out against one's true wishes, but service performed with love and inner identification. The feeling that should accompany the fulfillment of *mitzvot* should be harmony on all planes: intellect, emotion, imagination and desire.

Rejoicing in the mitzvot is connected to the Redemption

Deep identification with the *mitzvot* of the Torah is the hope of the future. This is what our Sages meant when they said, "*Mitzvot* will be nullified at the time of the Redemption."[22] This means that we will keep all the *mitzvot* not because we are commanded to do so by a force external to ourselves, but rather because we choose to do so as a natural expression of our inner desires.[23] Already today, this has come partially true. For example, most of us are not murderers. Is this because the Torah forbids murder? No! It's because we are not capable of murder; it goes against our nature. If one of us murders inadvertently, he or she is likely to die of anguish as a result. One can go so far as to say that the commandment, "Thou shalt not murder," is completely superfluous for most of us today. As a result of thousands of years of instruction, this precept has become second nature. An explicit commandment is no longer necessary.

So it will be with all the *mitzvot*. We hope to reach a point where, as a result of ongoing education, all the *mitzvot* become second nature, and we will fulfill them intuitively, without the need for instruction. This can be likened to an infant who nurses instinctively and has no need for lessons on the value of mother's milk. The educational role played by the performance of *mitzvot* is not meant to foist upon us values which are incompatible with our nature. On the contrary, the *mitzvot* are intrinsically well-suited to us, and ultimately this truth will emerge from behind the veil which now it.

Our Sages teach, "Had the *mitzvot* not been written in the Torah, we would have learned modesty from the cat, chastity from the dove," and so on.[24] This teaches us that the *mitzvot* as desirable modes of behavior are an integral part of Creation, and even appear, to a certain extent, in the animal world. Likewise, the Sages teach that our forefathers, Avraham, Yitzchak and Yaakov, observed the Torah in its entirety even before it was revealed.[25] How is this possible? It is because their sense of morality was so well-developed that they intuitively understood what they should and should not do. They fulfilled all the *mitzvot* naturally, requiring no explicit commandments.[26] We, today, have to understand that the *mitzvot* guide us towards our true inner nature that will be revealed in the World to Come. At that time, we will fulfill the *mitzvot* with joy and will experience a deep connection with them.

Simchat Torah: The Essence of *Am Yisrael*

Our sages explain that the verse, "And you shall *only* rejoice,"[27] teaches us that we should include the last day of Sukkot – Shemini Atzeret – in the *mitzva* of rejoicing, as on the other days of Sukkot.[28] This idea presents a difficulty because it is known that the word "only" always connotes exclusion, not inclusion. The Vilna Gaon resolved the matter by explaining that the word "only" refers here to the idea that on Shemini Atzeret there is no special *mitzva* other than to rejoice – i.e., all other *mitzvot* are excluded except for that of rejoicing.

Our Sages provided us with a parable to help us understand the essence of Shemini Atzeret: A king holds a big festive banquet and invites everyone. At the end of the meal, he requests his closest friends to remain another day in order to have an intimate, private banquet. To a certain extent, the festival of Sukkot belongs to all the nations, as we see in the *haftara* of the first day of Sukkot where it is mentioned that God will punish those nations who don't come to celebrate Sukkot at the End of Days. In addition, the seventy oxen offerings of the festival[29] correspond to the seventy nations of the world. Then, after seven days with all the nations, God requests *Am Yisrael* to dine alone with him.

On Shemini Atzeret, *Am Yisrael'*s own unique character finds expression. It can therefore be understood why, over the centuries, the *simcha* of Shemini Atzeret has come to be merged with Simchat Torah.[30] According to Rabbi Saadia Gaon, "Our nation is not a nation without its Torah" – the Torah is the deepest possible expression of the essence of *Am Yisrael'*s soul.

Does Am Yisrael precede the Torah or does the Torah precede Am Yisrael?

We may ask: Is the basic nature of *Am Yisrael* determined by the observance of Torah and *mitzvot*, or is the reverse true – that the very essence of *Am*

Yisrael precedes the Torah and it is this essence which requires that we observe Torah and *mitzvot*? The answer can be found in our Sages' formulation of the blessing over the Torah, "who has chosen us from all the nations and given us His Torah." The uniqueness of *Am Yisrael* – which is in itself the result of Divine creation and chosenness – is the reason that we were elected to receive the Torah. As our Sages recount, God offered the Torah to all the nations of the world, but *Am Yisrael* was the only nation who agreed to receive it. According to *Maharal* of Prague, this *midrash* expresses the idea that the Torah is incompatible with the character of all the other nations.[31]

Eliyahu Hanavi tells us of a man who had a dilemma: He cherished two things – the Torah and *Am Yisrael* – and he didn't know which one should take precedence. Eliyahu told him, "Most people say that the Torah is first, but I'll tell you the truth. *Am Yisrael* is first." The Torah is the instrument through which the Divine nature of the soul of *Am Yisrael* can express itself.

However, this nature is not always apparent to all; it may be concealed by our failure to observe Torah and *mitzvot*. Nevertheless, it is eternal – as everything Divine is eternal – as it says in *Shmuel*, "The Eternal God of Israel will neither lie nor change His mind."[32] All Jews are inextricably connected to their Divine source, however unaware of it they may be. As the prophet Yeshayahu states: "One will say, 'I am for God,' and another will be called by the name Yaakov; one will sign his hand to God, and [another] will be called by the name Yisrael."[33] There are those Jews who clearly identify themselves as "for God" and who "sign [their] hand to God"; there are others who lack this commitment, but who can nevertheless be called "by the name Yaakov" and "by the name Yisrael," for they have a strong Jewish identity.

The unique nature of *Am Yisrael* finds expression in the *mesirut nefesh*, the devotion and self-sacrifice, with which we have built up *Eretz Yisrael* and continue to defend it. This *mesirut nefesh* is also manifested in the fierce protection of our fellow Jews, whether within *Eretz Yisrael* or by bringing Jews from hostile countries to *Eretz Yisrael*. We do not attempt to deny our shortcomings in Torah observance, for God will search it out, and He knows the secrets of the heart. Mankind sees the obvious shortcomings, but our Creator understands us in depth[34] and knows that even in these situations we still cling to Him, as it says in *Tehillim*, "For we have been killed for Your sake all the days."[35] Our *mesirut nefesh* to sanctify His name, His land

and His nation, even to the point of death, is the greatest testimony to our fundamental devotion to God.

This is what Shemini Atzeret signifies – a joy beyond all specific and formal definition, an unbounded delight not confined to the performance of any specific *mitzva*: "Only rejoice." The *Arizal* says that on this festival, we should dance and sing in honor of the Torah with all our might,[36] as King David did in Jerusalem.[37] He is even said to have ascribed his exceptional achievements in understanding the secrets of the Torah to the great joy which he expressed on Simchat Torah.

Chanuka
Contemplating Miracles

Realism or Faith: Reflections on Chanuka

ACCORDING TO BOTH the Book of Maccabees and Josephus Flavius, the army of Yehuda HaMaccabee numbered no more than a few thousand soldiers at the beginning of the revolt. Why were Yehuda HaMaccabee's supporters so few in number? Where were all the Jews who lived in *Eretz Yisrael* then? Surely not all of them had assimilated into Greek culture! Why then did they not join the forces of rebellion? Didn't all of *Am Yisrael* yearn for national and spiritual freedom?

The Book of Maccabees describes the debates between Yehuda HaMaccabee and his soldiers, who claimed that there was simply no chance that the tiny, ill-equipped and inexperienced forces of *Am Yisrael* could defeat the mighty Greek army.[1] In addition, the revolt could have endangered the whole nation. This was no mere personal risk-taking: by raising the flag of rebellion, the Maccabees were inviting the Greek rulers to take revenge upon all of *Am Yisrael*, in the same way that the Greeks had responded to other rebellious provinces and cities.[2] Furthermore, Yehuda HaMaccabee was a self-appointed leader; the Maccabees were not the official leaders of *Am Yisrael*. Thus, there was no democratic decision or general consensus on the part of the people to declare a rebellion.

Of course, it is certain that Yehuda HaMaccabee was fully aware of all of the above and wasn't any less of a realist than those who challenged him. He was, perhaps, even more aware than they were of the military odds. However, he also had a clear sense of Jewish history. He reminded his soldiers that if we had been "realistic" in past generations, we never would have left Egypt, nor would David have taken on Goliath, nor Yonatan the Philistines.

As narrated in the Book of Maccabees, Yehuda HaMaccabee saw the mighty Greek forces and prayed: "Blessed are You, the Savior of Israel, who silenced the anger of the mighty through Your servant David, and who delivered the Philistine camp into the hands of Yonatan, son of Shaul, and his arm-bearer. Please deliver this camp into the hands of Your people Israel."[3]

In previous generations, there had always been a prophet to assure the people that God was with them. But at the time of Chanuka, the Maccabees had to have simple faith in God. Nowadays, we are accustomed to speaking about our faith in God, about Divine providence and God's hand directing history. But the Maccabees did not merely proclaim their faith; they lived it.

Yehuda HaMaccabee had no guarantee that he would be successful, nor did he promise victory to his forces. He simply said, "It is better for us to die in battle than to see evil triumph over our people and our *Beit HaMikdash*, and may the Lord do as He sees fit."[4] In other words, there is no assurance of victory, but we must fight nevertheless. It is neither futile nor hopeless, for there is a fair chance we will win. There have been times in our history when the few vanquished the many. We must fulfill our duty: if we are victorious, well and good; if not, it is God's will. Neither can we be considered to be recklessly endangering our lives in the expectation that God will perform a miracle to save us. A military victory is definitely within the realm of possibility, as a result of superior motivation, tactics, mobility, and knowledge of the terrain.

Thus, what Yehuda HaMaccabee teaches us is that our connection to God is not merely an interesting philosophical subject. It is a living reality that must be incorporated into our political and military planning. That was the first time since prophecy had ceased that someone arose and declared: "Belief in God is not merely theoretical. It bears practical implications. It gives me the strength, and even the imperative, to go to war." The miraculous-natural victory of the Maccabees does indeed make clear, once and for all, that faith in God is the noblest and most omnipresent realism of all.

The Maccabees' Revolt

Underground resistance of Yehuda HaMaccabee

How did Yehuda HaMaccabee dare to act without the support of the whole nation? Who appointed him king or authorized him to declare war? R. Avraham Yitzchak Kook raises this question and replies:

The fundamental issue for which the Maccabees fought was freedom of religion. The Greeks attempted "to make them forget Your Torah and to transgress the laws You desire them to follow."[5] Under such a threat (*shemad*) we are commanded to die rather than transgress even the smallest commandment. Therefore, isn't it not only permitted, but an obligation, to fight in order to put an end to this religious persecution and restore freedom of religion?[6]

In other words, the Maccabees' revolt did not begin as a war, but rather as an underground resistance to persecution, and intensified to the point that they were endangering their lives in order to sanctify God's name (known in Hebrew as *mesirut nefesh al kiddush Hashem*).

Indeed, we are commanded to sacrifice our lives in order to preserve our freedom to worship God. However, if we can kill our persecutors instead of forfeiting our lives, all the better. We are not obliged to allow ourselves to be killed if we can defend ourselves. Certainly, then, organizing an armed resistance which may deter our enemies from persecuting and killing us in the future is a great *mitzva*. This resistance is not considered a full-fledged war, but rather is the individual obligation of each Jew. There is, therefore, no need for a national consensus – although every individual member of *Am Yisrael* is obligated to act in such a manner.

Armed resistance on Shabbat

This approach provides insight into another issue. In the beginning of the Greek persecution, many Jews fled to caves in the wilderness, and the Greeks would come to attack them on Shabbat. The besieged Jews refused to desecrate Shabbat by counter-attacking the Greeks or even by blocking off the entrances to their caves. They, their wives and children were killed. When Matityahu and his group heard this, they grieved and said, "If we continue this trend...we will all be wiped out.... If our enemies come to fight us on Shabbat, we shall fight back and defend ourselves. We will not allow them to kill us as they did our brothers in the caves."[7]

This passage is puzzling: Didn't the Jews in the caves know that saving a life takes precedence over Shabbat observance, thereby permitting one to fight on Shabbat? It's hard to believe that this *halacha* was originated by Matityahu HaChashmonai. Did all previous wars in *Eretz Yisrael* – during the days of Yehoshua, King David, and so on – end every Friday before sundown? In the case of these Jews, we may deduce that they did not view their underground learning of Torah as a form of resistance against the Greeks. Rather, they were risking their lives in order to observe the Torah. It was for the purpose of keeping the *mitzvot* that they had fled to the wilderness.[8]

It was for this reason that they refused to fight on Shabbat. They viewed the Greek attacks on Shabbat as part of their general attempt to coerce the Jews into transgressing the Torah. Thus, they chose to die rather than desecrate the Shabbat.[9]

In response, Matityahu and his group initiated a new principle: The fight to preserve the Torah and *mitzvot* would from now on no longer be passive, because this line of action would lead to the extermination of *Am Yisrael*. Instead, they would actively resist, through warfare, the Greeks' oppressive laws against them. The Maccabees saw combat as a legitimate and effective method of preventing Greek religious persecution. They were committed to active resistance, which could very well entail fighting on Shabbat. Engaging in war on Shabbat is permitted according to *Halacha*; one is even obligated to desecrate Shabbat in order to save a Jewish soul.[10]

Was the Maccabees' war mandatory?

There is another puzzling fact: Yehuda HaMaccabee exempted from his "army" all the categories of people that are exempted by the Torah.[11] However, the exemptions in *Devarim* refer to a voluntary war, whereas in a mandatory war, our Sages tell us that "everyone goes to war, even a bridegroom…."[12] Wasn't the Maccabees' war a mandatory one, stemming firstly from the obligation of saving *Am Yisrael* from foreign oppression (i.e., of rescuing Jews from death) and secondly from the obligation of conquering the Land (i.e., redeeming *Eretz Yisrael* from Greek rule and establishing Jewish sovereignty)? If the Maccabees' war was mandatory, how, then, could he have released any soldiers?

The explanation is that in the first stages of the revolt, it was not a halachically recognized war. Such a war can only be declared by the whole nation, represented by the king or some other head of state. *Eretz Yisrael* was, at the time, subservient to the Seleucid rulers and had no national institutions of its own from which to receive approval for the uprising. Yehuda HaMaccabee had not been chosen or appointed to represent the nation and therefore had no authority to declare war. The armed opposition was his own personal initiative. He was certain that this was the correct course of action and the one which would lead to the physical and spiritual salvation of *Am Yisrael*. However, he also knew that, at least at first, he did not have the support of the majority. He could not act in the name of *Am Yisrael* and could not exercise the authority of a ruler to declare war. Subsequently, as a result of the Maccabees' repeated victories in battle, they gradually won over the people until they were unanimously accepted as national leaders and kings.[13]

Therefore, although his armed resistance was indeed a *mitzva*, it was not considered a war since he did not represent the nation, and he could not recruit those who are required to fight only in a mandatory war. For the same reason, Yehuda HaMaccabee didn't conscript soldiers; he depended solely on volunteers for his "army." Only later, when the nation as a whole came to support the Maccabees, did the Hasmoneans exercise the authority of rulers.

Was the miracle of the oil necessary?

The oil that miraculously burned for eight days arouses many questions. What need was there for a miracle at all? According to *Halacha*, if there is no pure oil available, one is permitted to use impure oil. Furthermore, after so many years of the *menora* not having been lit, couldn't they simply have waited a few more days to light it with pure oil? In any case, what is there about this particular miracle that makes it worthy of its own holiday? Many miracles have been recorded in Jewish history, and most of them do not warrant setting aside a special holiday.

Maharal of Prague explains that the seemingly insignificant miracle of the flask of oil was a sign from God to those who were doubtful that He endorsed the Maccabees. The miracle served to publicize to all that the Maccabees' war against the Greeks was in line with God's will, and that, from beginning to miraculous end, the whole process was a result of Divine providence and direction: "And therefore the candles burned miraculously, in order for all to know that God had performed miracles throughout, and that the [Maccabees'] victory in war was effected by the Holy One."[14]

According to some commentators, the first of the eight days of Chanuka is celebrated in honor of the military victory and the actual discovery of the flask of pure oil, and the other seven days in honor of the miracle of the oil burning continuously.[15] The other opinions hold that no special day was set aside to commemorate the victory. Their rationalization is that the miracle of the oil itself is none other than an affirmation of the miraculous nature of the military victory, as we have said above.

A clear, Divine stamp of approval

The fact that we can analyze the logistics and military strategy of every battle does not contradict the idea of Divine intervention. After hundreds of years of dependence and restrictions, it is miraculous that the Maccabees had the wisdom and courage to fight as they did.[16] This is a subtle, concealed miracle, however, which leaves people free to claim that the victory in war was natural. Therefore, God caused the oil to burn miraculously for eight days, in order to give a clear Divine stamp of approval to the whole physical and spiritual struggle.

It was only at the end, after the Maccabees had fought and won, that everyone realized that God was with them and that they were accepted as national leaders.[17] Although the Torah teaches us that a king must be "chosen by the Lord your God,"[18] this need not necessarily be through the words of a prophet. Unqualified success in redeeming *Am Yisrael* is in itself a clear sign from God that a leader has been chosen. The Hasmonean kings were appointed by the *Sanhedrin* rather than by a prophet, since prophecy had ceased in their generation. Gradually, through their devotion to God and their remarkable achievements, the Maccabees won the hearts of *Am Yisrael* and attained positions of leadership, one after another. First Yehuda HaMaccabee led the nation, then Yonatan, then Shimon – at which point he was officially given the title *"Nassi,"* and the Hasmonean family were established as rulers.

Making Miracles Happen
Does God Need Our Help?

THE STORY IS TOLD of a minor incident which occurred at the end of the Yom Kippur War, when forces commanded by General Ariel Sharon finally succeeded in entrapping Egypt's Third Army. A religious, bearded soldier approached a group of non-observant soldiers with a tremulous but enthusiastic smile on his face. One of the soldiers cut him off before he could open his mouth and said, "I know what you're going to say – that we won because of God's miracles – but it's not true; if I hadn't aimed my cannon well, no one would have aimed it for me!"

Despite the logic of this soldier's words, the *Al HaNissim* prayer recited on Chanuka asserts that we give thanks for this miracle – the miracle of the military and political victories wrought by the Maccabees. On the other hand, when the Talmud asks, "What is Chanuka?" it mentions only the heaven-sent miracle of the oil burning for eight days.[19] Is there any message behind this dichotomy? What is the relationship between "natural" miracles, apparently performed by humans, and those sent from above which seemingly defy nature?

Heroism is in itself a miracle

The nature of miracles is examined in a number of places in the Talmud. In Tractate *Berachot*, R. Pappa wants to know why miracles were prevalent during R. Yehuda's time, even though the latter generation was inferior in both

Torah study and prayer. Abaye answers: As opposed to us, our predecessors exemplified self-sacrifice (*mesirut nefesh*) in order to sanctify God's name.[20] It would seem, then, that the bravery and heroism of the Maccabees somehow indirectly contributed to the miracle of the Chanuka oil!

How do we know that the sudden appearance of this kind of heroism is in itself a miracle? In Tractate *Bava Metzia*, the following case is discussed: A shepherd walked away from his flock, which was later attacked by a lion and a bear. Had he been there, we certainly wouldn't have expected him to try and overpower these animals. Nevertheless, the possibility is raised that had he been on duty, a miracle might have taken place, as it did for King David when he overpowered a lion and a bear.[21] *Tosafot* explain that the miracle that could have taken place is that he would have been miraculously infused with a "spirit of heroism," thus enabling him to overpower the attackers.[22]

From these two sources, we see that heroism beyond the call of duty is, on the one hand, a miracle in and of itself, and on the other hand, can also be the catalyst for other miracles.

Everything can be seen as a miracle

A different aspect of miracles is discussed in Tractate *Ta'anit*. Chanina ben Dosa was a great *tzaddik* who was so poor that his embarrassed wife used to make her oven smoke on Fridays so that the neighbors would think she had *challa* to bake. Once, when she was challenged by a neighbor to open her oven, lo and behold, it was miraculously filled with steaming, fragrant *challa*. The surprised neighbor quickly asked for a baker's spatula to remove the *challot*. The Talmud comments that Mrs. ben Dosa had the baker's spatula ready because she was accustomed to living with miracles! The Talmud goes on to list a number of such miracles, including one where Chanina ben Dosa's wife cried out that she had mistakenly poured vinegar into the Shabbat candelabra instead of oil. Her husband answered, "Don't worry – He who commanded oil to burn can command vinegar to burn as well!"[23]

This story stresses an important point. The vast cosmos is miraculous; the tiny working organs of bacteria are miraculous; and so is everything in between. All events – whether internal or external, whether they fit today's conception of the laws of nature or not – are a miracle from God. The word for miracle in Hebrew is *ness*, which also means "flag" or "banner" – something that can be seen from afar. Everything in this world is a miracle; we just have to recognize and appreciate it as such.

Many of our most dedicated brothers and sisters do not recognize the miraculous nature of the return to *Eretz Yisrael*. Before sending off his students to settle in *Eretz Yisrael*, the Vilna Gaon predicted this situation. He told them that the word "Zion" and the word "Yosef" have the same *gematria* (numerical value) – 156. During the season of Chanuka, we read the portions of the Torah dealing with Yosef who, when reunited with his family, was not initially recognized by his brothers. In the same way, when the light of Redemption in Zion begins to shine, it will not be recognized by many of our fellow Jews.

We find a similar phenomenon occurring during the time of Mordechai and Esther. The Talmud explains the passage in *Megillat Esther* which says that "Mordechai was accepted by *most* of his brothers"[24] by pointing out that not all Jews agreed with Mordechai's policy of heroism in not bowing down to Haman.[25] The same problem occurred during the Maccabean Revolt when many Jews refused to recognize the leadership role of the Maccabees and didn't believe that they could vanquish the Greek king. Here, too, the Hebrew words for "Greek king" – *Melech Yavan* – equal the *gematria* of 156!

Returning for a moment to the stories of Chanina ben Dosa, these stories should not be taken literally but rather should be appreciated for their deeper meaning. There is a concept in Kabbala called *Nahama DeKisufa*, or the bread of shame. It isn't a coincidence that this term is used for the bread which appeared miraculously for Chanina ben Dosa's wife. This kabbalistic term helps us to understand why God doesn't miraculously provide us with all His bounty without requiring us to make our own independent efforts. God wants to do what is ultimately good for us, but, in order to receive His gifts, we must earn them, so that there will be no shame attached to what we receive from Him. This is the basis for the give-and-take relationship between God and mankind.

Sukkot and Chanuka

The many interesting parallels that exist between Sukkot and Chanuka are well known. Both are eight days long; both the *sukka* and the Chanuka lights are limited to a 20-cubit height; both candles and *sukka* decorations are forbidden to be used for other purposes; and the progression of the number of sacrifices on Sukkot resembles the progression of the number of candles lit per night (according to Beit Shammai).

This parallelism was taken one step further by the *Sefat Emet* who, back in 1881, before anyone ever dreamed of Yom HaAtzmaut, made an interesting classification of our holidays: There were three decreed by God, and for each one there is an analogous holiday decreed by *Am Yisrael*:

- On Shavuot, God gave us the Torah by force (as the Talmud tells us, "God threatened them by holding Mount Sinai above them like a basin, saying, 'If you agree to accept the Torah, fine, and if not, here will be your burial place'"[26]). On Purim we, of our own volition, reaffirmed our acceptance of the Torah (as *Megillat Esther* states, "The Jews carried out and accepted the Torah"[27]).
- On Sukkot, God defended us; on Chanuka we defended ourselves.
- On Pesach, God liberated us; on the future "*Chag HaGeula*," we will liberate ourselves.

All these holidays celebrate miracles: the holidays decreed by God honor the supernatural miracles performed by Him, whereas the rabbinical holidays, ordained by *Am Yisrael*, mark those miracles brought about by humans.

The purpose of the miracle of the oil

As we explained earlier, the fact that the oil lasted for eight days seems, on the face of it, to be an unnecessary miracle, and certainly not one which would warrant the declaration of a holiday. The answer provided by *Maharal* is that God performed the miracle of the oil in order to signal his approval of the actions of the Maccabees – who were *Kohanim* and not from the House of David, as kings should be – in leading the battle and eventually establishing a monarchy.

When we give a present, we don't give a sack of potatoes, but rather flowers or something else that isn't necessary useful but is beautiful – something symbolic which conveys our emotions. The miracle of the oil was superfluous, but it symbolized God's endorsement of the Hasmonean Dynasty. Oil was chosen to be the vehicle of the miracle because oil was used to anoint the Kings of Israel and lies at the root of the word *Mashiach* (lit., "anointed with oil").

The answers to our questions are now clear. Since prayer is our way of communicating with God, in the prayer "*Al HaNissim*" we make reference to the miracle of the fighting which we ourselves carried out. As we saw in *Bava Metzia*, in the case discussed above, human heroism is in itself a miracle. On the other hand, studying Torah is our way of delving into God's words, of listening for His response. In the Talmud, therefore, the focus is on the miracle of the oil, which was God's response to the self-sacrifice of the Maccabees.

There is not always a logical connection between how we struggle and sacrifice ourselves for a cause and the manner in which we are answered. The self-sacrifice is our "*hishtadlut*" – our duty to make an effort – but God will answer us as He sees fit. The only thing we can be sure about is that we *will* be answered. If we go about our lives doing only the minimum expected of us, then God will do no more for us than is consistent with nature. If we, on the other hand, make tremendous efforts and sacrifices, if we brave difficult situations and hardships, if we make a superhuman effort, then we will be rewarded with some form of supernatural response or miracle.

This non-causal connection between our actions and God's salvation is clear from the words of the Maccabees: "It is better for us to die in battle than to see evil triumph over our people and our *Beit HaMikdash*, and may the Lord do as He sees fit."[28] Yoav, the chief of staff of King David's army, uses a similar phrase, "Be strong for our people and the cities of our God, and may the Lord do as He sees fit."[29] Someone once phrased it this way: Don't give God instructions – just show up for duty!

Heroism in our generation

The ultimate place both for acts of self-sacrifice and for miracles is Jerusalem. It all started long before the time of the Maccabees, at the dawn of *Am Yisrael*'s history. This is why the story of the *Akeida* – the sacrifice of Yitzchak – took place in Jerusalem. Here too, it was Avraham's willingness to sacrifice his son that earned him his elevated status. In this case as well, the results were not the expected ones and Yitzchak lived on.

We said earlier that Sukkot is comparable to Chanuka. The passage in Tehillim, "His *sukka* was in Shalem, and his dwelling place in Zion," was explained by the Vilna Gaon to mean that just like a *sukka* must be built with human hands, so must Zion be built through our own efforts, without waiting for heavenly miracles. If we initiate actions here on earth – "an awakening from below" – then God will also bring about an "awakening from above." There is a saying in the *Zohar* and the Talmud, "The Lord swore He will not enter into the Jerusalem of Above until *Am Yisrael* enters the Jerusalem of Below."[30] If we strive to build and settle Jerusalem, then God will answer us by bringing salvation.

This, then, is the basic underlying philosophy of the settlement movement. We can make miracles happen; yet we also must be aware of the miracles all around us. The reason we settle territory is not that we are better political analysts than successive prime ministers, for we can never be sure of all of the ramifications of our actions. We do so because the same One who commanded us to sanctify the Shabbat commanded us to treasure the Land, His gift to His people. It is because the same One who commanded us to love all mankind, and especially our fellow Jews of all persuasions, taught us that if we show heroism and dedication, He will respond with some kind of miracle – all we have to do is look for it.

If all of creation is God's handiwork, then we would be blind not to see His miraculous hand in all that has befallen us in *Eretz Yisrael*. The great heroic spirit of self-sacrifice was miraculously reborn in people who weren't necessarily religious. They bravely decided to establish a state under the most difficult of conditions, and were faced with great opposition from within and from without. They came and settled, and fought and won, and God responded. The prophet Yechezkel said, "And you, the hills of Israel, give forth your branches and lift up your fruit for my people Israel, for they hasten to come."[31] The Talmud expounds on this verse, teaching that there is no greater revelation of the arrival of the *Mashiach* than the physical flowering of *Eretz Yisrael*.[32] The entire world today has long recognized the miracle of taming the deserts, of drying up the swamps, of tiny *Eretz Yisrael* turning itself into an agricultural superpower. After 2,000 years, the hills of *Eretz Yisrael* have become green again.

During this troubled period, it is difficult to appreciate the miracles that God has showered upon us. It takes the Festival of Lights to remind us, in these dark times, that no matter what the odds are, Jewish courage and fortitude can, and will, prevail.

The Holocaust

The Holocaust According to *Aish Kodesh*

Two books were written about the Holocaust in the depths of that terrible era. Their authors were great rabbis who themselves were martyred *al kiddush Hashem* – to sanctify God's name. One is *Eim HaBanim Semeicha* by R. Yissachar Teichtal,[1] and the other is *Aish Kodesh*, by the *Admor* of Piaseczna, R. Kalonymus Kalmish Shapiro, may God avenge their deaths. The latter manuscript was discovered in an urn buried in the ruins of the Warsaw Ghetto and brought to the Historical Institute of Warsaw. It consists of *parashat shavua derashot* – sermons on the weekly Torah portion – given by R. Shapiro in the ghetto from 1939 until 1942.

Eim HaBanim Semeicha explains that suffering and the birth pangs of the *Mashiach* are preparations for the universal *tikkun* (remedy) of building the nation, achieving unity in *Am Yisrael* and going to live in *Eretz Yisrael*. In contrast, *Aish Kodesh* deals with the *tikkun* of the individual: how suffering can help us overcome the impure forces that surround us, and how to grow in purity and holiness. There is, obviously, no contradiction between the *tikkun* of the individual and the *tikkun* of the nation, but it is important to note that each book emphasizes a different aspect. Most of what appears below concerning the acceptance of suffering and justice is taken directly from *Aish Kodesh*.

God reveals Himself through the concealing veil of misfortune

"Out of suffering I cried to God; God answered me with good fortune."[2] It is precisely in times of suffering that an exceptional Divine light appears to us. The more intense the suffering, the greater the Divine light which then shines upon us.

This may be compared to a king's son who was taken captive by thugs and tortured. He sensed that the king was nearby and so began to cry out, "Save me, my father; save me, my king!" He cried out only because he felt the proximity of his father. So, too, when Jews' hearts are overwhelmed by their own personal suffering and that of *Am Yisrael*, this testifies to our closeness to God. This is only the case, of course, if our afflictions bring us a greater fear of God and a greater desire to acknowledge His sovereignty. Therefore, almost paradoxically, we find that the hiddenness of God is actually a special type of revelation: We are brought to a level of terrible suffering, and suddenly we feel closer to God and perceive that He is close to us.[3]

Salvation follows suffering

Yaakov fought all through the night with an angel who represented Eisav. Finally, Yaakov told him, "I shall not release you until you bless me."[4] Why did Yaakov need the angel's blessing? Wasn't the blessing he had already received from God sufficient?

The answer is that "the deeds of the forefathers are a sign and precedent for their sons."[5] When the struggle ended with Yaakov injured, the angel attempted to leave him. However, Yaakov said to himself: "Is this what will happen to my sons? After they suffer adversity, will their deliverance merely be that they remain undefeated and return to their previous state? Shouldn't they gain something from all their misfortunes?" Therefore he said, "I shall not release you until you bless me." These travails must culminate in a deliverance which elevates the sufferer and does not only bring about an end to affliction.[6]

Suffering is chesed concealed

From the Divine point of view, even the worst misfortunes are *chesed* (loving-kindness), albeit of a concealed nature. We should strive to make ourselves one with God's "thoughts" and then to filter them down, into this world, through speech and action. It is then that God's compassion will also be apparent, and not just His judgment and the concealment of His *chesed*.[7] We must understand that suffering is in itself *chesed*. When we achieve this understanding, our suffering becomes beneficial to us. However, if we cannot comprehend this, then our suffering really does not bring anything but misfortune.

God's strict justice is actually more exalted than His mercy, but it is very difficult for us, in the here and now, to comprehend and accept this. We are not strong enough to face judgment, and so it appears to us as punishment. The *Midrash* tells us that at the time of Creation, when God saw that mankind would not survive in a world based only on strict justice (*din*), He tempered it with mercy.[8] In our world, the *Kohanim* serve in the *Beit HaMikdash* and we follow the judgments of *Beit Hillel* in *Halacha*. Both the *Kohanim* and *Beit Hillel* represent mercy and leniency in judgment. But in the future ideal world, it is the *Levi'im* who will serve in the *Beit HaMikdash*, and we will follow the halachic judgments of *Beit Shammai*. Both the *Levi'im* and *Beit Shammai* represent strict justice.

In the future, we will comprehend how merciful strict justice really is, and how beneficial all the suffering of *Am Yisrael* has been. Today, when our world is still imperfect, and we are not ready for such a revelation, all this suffering appears to be a punishment. The prophets, who were able to view our troubles from above, could see how great was the Divine light imbued in them. We, who see the troubles from below, find it difficult to discern in them anything positive.

When Pharaoh's decrees became even harsher after Moshe and Aharon's first visit to him, Moshe asked God, "Why have you made things so much worse for this people?"[9] Such a question from a leader of Moshe's caliber comes as a surprise. Moshe, in fact, was protesting to God, "*I* know that this suffering is beneficial. But the common people, who cannot stand any more suffering or comprehend the good in it, why have you made things so much worse for *them?*" *Am Yisrael*'s mode of thinking then was similar to ours today. They hoped for redemption, and instead, conditions worsened, and they suffered even more. In other words, Moshe was saying that in absolute terms, great benefit resulted from *Am Yisrael*'s suffering, but the ordinary person was unable to detect it.[10]

The labor pains of the Mashiach

The pains leading up to the revelation of the *Mashiach* are akin to labor pains – birth emerging from suffering.[11] It is clear that our troubles result from the necessity to cleanse ourselves of our sins before the coming of the *Mashiach*. It is impossible to "give birth" – i.e., to serve as the agent in bringing new light into the world – without nullifying at least part of one's own light. Thus, the appearance of new light necessitates the nullification of the old one. Without *bitul hayesh*, nullification of one's existence, God's light cannot be revealed.

This well-known concept in *Chassidut* derives from *Maharal* of Prague, who comments on our Sages' statement that since the destruction of the *Beit HaMikdash*, "the Holy One has nothing in His treasury save a treasure of fear of God."[12] *Maharal* asks: Why is there only a treasure of fear of God, and not love of God, which is on a higher level? He goes on to explain that "love" means "I exist, and I love God." "Fear" means "I don't really exist. I nullify my existence when encountering the greatness of God." Therefore, if I wish to reveal the Divine light within myself, I must nullify myself.[13] As long as my "I" is still very present, I cannot receive the Divine light because my "I" is standing in its way.

In a similar vein, when a seed is planted, it first must rot in the ground. Only after it ceases to exist will a wonderful plant sprout from it. This plant will have leaves and branches and will bear fruit many times the size of the original seed. All this potential was hidden within the tiny seed, which first had to "die" in order for the new creation to be revealed.

Chava was cursed: "In pain shall you bear children."[14] This means that in order for her to give birth to a new being, her own strength had to be diminished. In order to become a mother, she had to sacrifice a part of her own self. The pains leading up to the *Mashiach* are similar. Redemption is a Divine revelation. The Holy One will reveal His light in the universe through *Am Yisrael*. In order for this great light to be revealed, we – the agents – must be diminished. These are the pains of the *Mashiach*.

In *Yeshayahu*, it is written, "Shall I induce labor (*ashbir*) and not bring about birth? asks God."[15] The word *ashbir* is similar to the word *mashber*, which means crisis. God induces labor and then He helps us to give birth. The greater the labor pains, the greater the light that they produce. The Jew who suffers terribly from the pains of the *Mashiach* is able to reveal more of the light of the *Mashiach*. These are the pains of disintegration for the sake of restoration, and not pain merely for the sake of pain. As the seed must rot before the tree can grow, and as a woman must labor before she can give birth, so must we undergo the pains of the *Mashiach* before Redemption can come. The Master of the World brings salvation through suffering. Therefore, we must accept these pains and understand their significance. We must not rebel against God, but rather perceive the mercy of His ways. This is an exalted form of mercy. We, who find ourselves in the midst of this, must realize that these are the pains of cleaving to God through nullifying our own existence.[16]

The above ideas represent a small sample of the writings of the Holy *Admor*, Rabbi Kalonymos Shapiro, may God avenge his death. There is nothing that can be added to them.[17]

Where was God during the Holocaust?

GOD WAS CERTAINLY PRESENT. Moreover, it was He who decided that there would be a Holocaust. Was it the Germans who determined the course of events, with the Master of the Universe impotent and unaware? No, it was God who decided. Why? This, we do not know. It is just as mysterious as when God decided that Chmielnicki would murder thousands of Jews, or that in Egypt, infants would be thrown into the Nile.[18]

God decreed that there would be a Holocaust, and He established the principle that "Good is carried out by the righteous, and evil is carried out by the wicked."[19] The Master of the Universe decided that we would leave Egypt and that His emissary would be Moshe. If His emissary had not been Moshe, it would have been someone else. In the same way, He would have found someone else to bring down the Torah from Mount Sinai, and He would have found a replacement for Yehuda HaMaccabee. If not for R. Yehuda HaNassi, would the entire Mishna have been lost? God forbid! Another emissary of God would have preserved it.

When Papos and Lulianus were caught by Trinanus, the latter said to them, "If there be a God, let Him perform a miracle for you as He did for Chanania, Mishael and Azaria in the fiery furnace!" They replied, "We are not righteous like they were, and you, too, are less worthy than was Nebuchadnezzar. Apparently, the Master of the Universe has decreed our death. If you do not kill us, God has many emissaries, many snakes and many scorpions, many lions and many leopards. Good is carried out by the righteous, and evil is carried out by the wicked."[20]

Whether God decides to treat us benevolently or otherwise, there are

70

always volunteers to implement it. Yet we do not know why God decided on a Holocaust. There are many things we do not know. Even *Rashi* very often writes in his Torah commentary, "I do not know its meaning."

Sometimes the handwriting of history is so blurred that we cannot decipher it. At other times, it is clear. What has been happening in our Land over the last hundred years is crystal clear. God has decided to bring salvation to His people "gradually."[21] Certainly we can see a connection between the Holocaust, which uprooted *Am Yisrael* from exile, and their subsequently being planted in their Land. We see the fulfillment of the verse in *Yechezkel*, As I live, says God, surely with a mighty hand and with an outstretched arm, and with anger poured out, will I be King over you, and I will bring you out from the peoples and I will gather you out of the countries in which you are scattered."[22]

Still, the reason for the Holocaust remains unclear. Just as we do not know why a three-year-old child dies of an illness, we also do not understand the Holocaust. We do not know why righteous people die in car accidents. When a righteous man dies in that way, his death is a Holocaust for his wife – or perhaps worse, for the Holocaust struck a third of *Am Yisrael*, but that woman's husband was everything to her. In the future we will know. Right now we do not.

Our teacher, R. Zvi Yehuda Kook, offered the following parable: a small boy is outside in a dangerous forest. His mother has made the house warm and prepared delicious food and although she calls him home, he does not come. Then she goes outside and pulls him in by force, and he gets caught on rocks and thorns, and arrives home bloody and battered. Yet he is home. He is alive and "he owes his life to his blood."[23]

One might ask: Does God not have other ways than this? Certainly He does. He has an infinite number of ways open to Him. We do not know why He chose this path and not another. Only with hindsight do we sometimes understand God's deeds. Sometimes we do not, but nevertheless we place our faith in Him.

Tu Bishvat

Planting Trees
A Universal Value

THE TORAH COMMANDS US to "follow God...and cling to Him."[1] Our Sages ask:

> Is it really possible for a human being to "climb" up to heaven and "cling" to God, of whom it is written, "For God is an all-consuming fire?"[2] Rather, the Torah is telling us to emulate the *middot* (character traits) of God. When God first created the world, He was occupied with planting trees, as it is written, "And God planted a garden in Eden."[3] So, too, when you enter *Eretz Yisrael,* make sure you occupy yourselves first with planting trees, as it is written, "And when you have come to the land, and you have planted all manner of trees for food...." [*Vayikra* 19:23][4]

Thus, God teaches us to plant trees by setting an example for us in the Garden of Eden. This is what the story of God planting a garden in Eden teaches us. This ideal is not necessarily only a Jewish one; it is universal. Human beings must make positive contributions to society and to the world at large: not only in agriculture, but also in science, industry, construction, and in establishing norms of productive interpersonal relationships. In other words, one must be involved in areas which bring benefit to mankind and to the world as a whole. Idleness indicates a flawed personality. It is for this reason that according to *Halacha*, chronic gamblers are unacceptable as witnesses in court.[5]

Attributing human characteristics to God

Some might ask such philosophical questions as: How did God plant trees? Isn't this an anthropomorphic description? Whenever the Torah mentions God's deeds, it is not actually describing Him, but rather talking to us, about us. We are completely incapable of understanding anything about God Himself or about His deeds, in and of themselves. All we can comprehend is how His deeds reveal themselves in the world to us.[6]

The same principle applies to social interaction. We can never objectively assess who another person really is; we can only describe how that person appears to us. All our relationships with the world and with one another are subjective and therefore biased. We cannot grasp the true essence of anything, but only our impressions of it. How much more so is this true of our comprehension of God and His deeds. All we can do is attempt to decipher the significance of God's deeds for us. Therefore, when the Torah writes, for example, that God had mercy, it doesn't mean that He felt the emotion that we call mercy. It merely means that from our perspective, we observed an act of mercy, which is a human quality. Feelings and deeds are attributed to God in order to teach human beings how to behave.

Little children think in absolute terms.[7] They think that what they understand is the unconditional, objective truth. The more mature we become, the more we understand how subjective our opinions are and how they represent only our conception of the world. We must help our children make this necessary transition. They must come to understand that we cannot describe God Himself, but only our subjective perception of Him. If this essential transition does not occur, then when they grow up, they are in danger of losing their faith in God, or of having a warped or misguided religious attitude.

Similarly, when we read in the Torah that God planted a garden in Eden, we are not to interpret this literally but metaphorically: if we wish to cling to God's ways, we, too, must be involved in planting. To "cling" to God does not mean to seek mystical experiences for ourselves, but rather to imitate His ways. Thus, when the Torah teaches us that God "planted a garden of trees," we deduce that it is His will that the earth be settled. It is His desire that we not be idle, but rather occupy ourselves with planting, building and the like in order to make the world a better place to live in.

The value of being involved in the physical world

This concept is diametrically opposed to Christian philosophy.[8] From a Christian perspective, the physical world is cursed; it is full of evil and suffering. Therefore, a priest who does not marry is to be admired, for why enlarge the numbers of poor, unfortunate creatures on this cursed earth? Judaism believes the opposite: this world is the "Garden of Eden,"[9] at least in potential and in essence. If it is not actually so today, that is the fault of mankind. We have spoiled it, but we can also restore the world and make it once again into a Garden of Eden. God, by planting a garden, teaches us that we must not develop only the spiritual world by studying Torah exclusively; rather, we must concurrently work at perfecting the material world. We must not belittle the physical, but rather enhance it, bringing it to perfection.

When we do so, we are following in God's footsteps. He made the heavens and the earth, created light, separated the dry land from the water, and established all the laws of nature. Our involvement with worldly matters should not be seen as a mere by-product of the need to earn a living (which is, in itself, a value). Rather, this occupation with the world is actually a lofty goal, provided that involvement with mundane concerns includes within it a desire to benefit the world. In every field, there are people whose achievements do not come from a desire to become famous, but rather from a sincere wish to contribute to society – for example, those who work to advance science or technology so that other people can live better lives. Another example is businessmen who are not interested only in their personal profit, but also in supplying goods based on consumer needs.[10]

So, too, the desire to plant trees reveals a wish to benefit others. The story is told of an aged man whom the Roman emperor found planting trees. The emperor asked him, "At your age, why are you planting? Do you really think you'll live to enjoy the fruit of these trees?" The old man answered, "If I do not live to enjoy the fruit, my children will!"[11] Planting trees, then, is a reflection of our idealism and holiness, for it is walking in the ways of God.[12] Just as God created the world and abolished chaos by establishing the laws of nature, so do we continue to bring order into chaos and to improve that which is still imperfect – and we are far from completing the job.[13] Thus, the desire to plant is an expression of man's inner desire to spread goodness and improve the world.

Purim

The Days of Purim Will Never Be Nullified

The future nullification of Scripture and the festivals

Rambam wrote in *Mishneh Torah:*

> All of the books of *Nevi'im* and *Ketuvim* will be nullified in the Messianic era except for *Megillat Esther*. It will exist as will the Five Books of the Torah and the precepts of the Oral Law, which will never be nullified. And even though the memory of the persecution will be nullified,[1] the days of Purim will not be nullified, as it says in *Megillat Esther*, "These days of Purim will never pass from the Jews and their memory will not cease from their descendants [9:28]."[2]

Two laws are presented here: 1) The rest of *Nevi'im* and *Ketuvim* will be nullified while *Megillat Esther* will not be nullified, and 2) All the holidays which commemorate persecution will be nullified, but the days of Purim will not.

The second law is perplexing. Why will the holidays that were established in order to commemorate persecution be nullified in the Messianic era? Even though the dangers themselves will have disappeared, surely it will be valuable to remember the salvation. Nowadays we continue to celebrate certain holidays in order to remind ourselves of times when God intervened to save us, even though those dangers have long passed. The answer lies in the difference between our times and the Messianic era. Although in our days we are free from the afflictions of old, we are still subject to other suffering. In the Messianic future, however, there will no persecution whatsoever, and therefore those holidays which serve to remind us of this aspect of our past need not be maintained.[3]

The first-mentioned law of *Rambam*, which says that the books of the *Nevi'im* and *Ketuvim* will be nullified – except for *Megillat Esther* – is even more perplexing. *Ravad* himself commented on *Rambam*, "No book of Scripture will be nullified, for there is no holy book from which we cannot learn." It is difficult to understand why *Rambam* wrote that the *Nevi'im* and *Ketuvim* will be nullified. However, *Rambam* did not invent this notion. His words are based on the *Talmud Yerushalmi*:

R. Yochanan said, "The *Nevi'im* and *Ketuvim* will be nullified in the future, but the Five Books of the Torah will never be nullified. What is the reason? 'A great voice which will not cease.' [*Devarim* 5:19]" R. Shimon ben Lakish said, "*Megillat Esther* and the Oral Law will not be nullified, for it said here [in reference to the Torah], 'A great voice which will not cease,' and it is said further on [in *Megillat Esther*], 'Their recollection will not cease from their descendants.'"[4]

If *Rambam's* words are based on the *Yerushalmi*, why does *Ravad* criticize him? *Ravad* interprets the word "nullify" differently: "But this is what they meant. Even if the other books will cease to be read in a formal public setting, *Megillat Esther* will never stop being read publicly." The rest of the *Nevi'im* and *Ketuvim* will no longer be used for the *haftarot*, but *Megillat Esther* will continue to be read publicly. The *Lechem Mishneh* interprets this passage similarly: "It doesn't mean that they will remove the other books, but rather that they will not be read on a fixed basis." This is also the understanding of the *Me'iri*: that the words of the *Yerushalmi* were meant figuratively, not literally. *Rambam*, however, took the *Yerushalmi* literally, and his words require explanation.

The *Maggid Mishneh* notes: "If the meaning of the text of the *Yerushalmi* is really literal as *Rambam* explains, then in the Messianic era, the truth will come to light." That is, since we are dealing with matters that are not currently relevant or practical, there is no need to resolve the issue now. Let us wait and see. When the *Mashiach* arrives, we will know the truth.

The Nevi'im and Ketuvim are included in the Five Books of the Torah

The Talmud discusses the principle that, "There is nothing written in the

Nevi'im and *Ketuvim* which is not alluded to in the Torah."[5] Indeed, we know that a prophet is not allowed to introduce anything new.[6]

The teachings of the prophets are hidden in the Torah and great understanding is needed in order to uncover them. The prophets came along and revealed, elaborated upon and explained that which was alluded to in the Torah. In the Messianic future, when "the earth shall be filled with the knowledge of the Lord"[7] and "no man shall teach his fellow,"[8] everyone will understand independently all that is written in the Torah. At that time, the *Nevi'im* and *Ketuvim* will be nullified. We will no longer need their words, for we will be able to interpret the prophetic allusions in the Torah on our own, without the explanations of the prophets.

In contrast, *Megillat Esther* will not be nullified because it is similar to the Torah and unlike the rest of *Nevi'im* and *Ketuvim*. The *Chatam Sofer* goes so far as to say that the light of the Torah of Moshe is included within *Megillat Esther*.[9] Just as the Torah itself will not be nullified, so, too, *Megillat Esther* will not be nullified.

The proof that *Megillat Esther* is like the Torah itself is found in the Talmud, where it is written that *Megillat Esther* requires lines etched on parchment like an actual Torah scroll.[10] That is to say, *Megillat Esther* is the only book that must be written like a Torah itself – on animal skin, with etched lines, and sewn together with sinew. Likewise, it must be read like the Torah. Just as the Torah is absolute and eternal truth, existing before the creation of the world and encompassing all generations, so, too, is *Megillat Esther* "words of peace and truth."[11] In contrast, the words of the prophets addressed specific periods and circumstances.

A further proof that *Megillat Esther* is like the Torah is found in the *Talmud Yerushalmi*: "*Megillat Esther* was said to Moshe at Sinai. Even though it doesn't appear that way in the Scripture, we know that the concept of chronological order doesn't apply to Scripture."[12] The *Megilla's* essential content, the Divine light within it, is from Sinai. At the giving of the Torah, the time had not yet come for it to be revealed, and so it was subsequently revealed in the days of Achashverosh.

We learn, therefore, that *Megillat Esther* shines as eternally as the Torah itself, in contrast to the *Nevi'im* and *Ketuvim*, which are not eternal. As our Sages said, "A prophecy which was required for all generations was recorded;

if it was not needed for future generations, it was not recorded."[13] Prophecies were given within specific contexts and situations, relating to the events and needs of that particular period. Those prophecies that contained teachings relevant for all future generations were written down. However, even these were originally said in the context of a specific time and place. Prophecy is not eternal; it is bound by time. Prophecy is referred to by the Talmud as "received words" (*divrei kabbala*), as opposed to the Torah of Moshe which is called "words of instruction" (*divrei Torah*).[14] *Rashi* explains, "The Torah of Moshe is called Torah (instruction) because the Torah was given for all generations. In contrast, the words of the prophets are only called *kabbala* (that which is received), for the prophets received each prophecy from the Holy Spirit according to the needs of each particular period and generation."[15]

It is worthwhile to try to understand the statement of our Sages:

> If Israel had not sinned they would only have received the Five Books of the Torah and the Book of *Yehoshua* (since the latter is the record of the arrangements of the tribal division of *Eretz Yisrael*). What is the reason for this? "For with much wisdom is much anger [*Kohelet* 1:18]."[16]

All of the wisdom that we merited to receive from the prophets came as a result of our sins which angered God. If it were not for this, we would not have needed the words of the prophets, and we would have received only the Torah and *Yehoshua*. Once we sinned, the prophets came to remind us of the words of the Torah, as did Malachi, the last of the prophets, who completes his prophecy with the words, "Remember the Torah of Moshe, My servant."[17]

Maharatz Chayos points to another aspect of the abolishment of the prophetic writings in the Messianic future and asks: "How is it possible that the words of the prophets will be nullified, for the Talmud records many laws which are derived from them, such as the laws of mourning from Yechezkel, the laws of prayer from Chana, and others? If the *Nevi'im* were nullified, from where would we learn these laws?"[18] He answers his question in accordance with the opinion of *Ramban*.[19] In truth, all the laws that were derived from the prophets – and were not previously mentioned – were received at Sinai and were transmitted from generation to generation, and were subsequently associated with verses from *Nevi'im*. This is in accordance with the words of our Sages, "Forty-eight prophets and seven prophetesses prophesied for Israel and they neither added nor subtracted to that which is in the Torah, except for the reading of the *Megilla*."[20] The prophets did not add any new laws; everything was given at Sinai.

This is, therefore, the proper way to understand the idea of the nullification of the prophetic writings in the Messianic future. These writings function only to reveal, elaborate upon and remind us of the Torah itself, in accordance with the particular needs of the time and the generation. In future days, when we will all be on a lofty level of intellectual and ethical perception, we will have no need for the writings of the prophets, for we will be independently capable of perceiving all the hidden aspects of the Torah and its allusions, and we will be loyal to God's word. *Megillat Esther*, however, is considered eternal truth, as is the Torah itself.

Divine kindness and Divine judgment

There is another explanation for the nullification of the *Nevi'im*, according to *Maharal* of Prague.[21] He explains that the words of the prophets convey Divine guidance arising from God's aspect of lovingkindness (*chesed*), a guidance which takes into account the circumstances of human weakness. In contrast, the words of the Torah stem from the aspect of strict judgment (*din*) – from the vantage point of absolute truth. In the Messianic future, when we will be on a higher spiritual plane, we will no longer need prophetic guidance based on a consideration of our limitations. We will, in fact, be able to be judged by the higher guidance of the Torah, which is absolute truth. Prophecy will certainly continue to exist as an eternal relationship between God and *Am Yisrael*. However, the actual words of the prophets will be obsolete, since we will be worthy of Divine guidance on the level of the Torah.

The light of the holidays of the present in contrast to the great light of the future

We have thus far explained the first *halacha* in the *Rambam's Mishneh Torah* – that the words of the *Nevi'im* and *Ketuvim* will be abolished in the Messianic era, in contrast to the continued existence of *Megillat Esther*.

Now we will explain the second *halacha*, which states that the holidays in the Messianic era will be nullified, as opposed to the days of Purim, which will never depart from the Jews. The source of this law is found in *Midrash Mishlei*:

> "The wise among women, each builds her house" and also "sets her table."[22] This refers to Queen Esther...she set her table in this world and for the World to Come, for all the holidays will be nullified but the days of Purim will never be nullified. Likewise, the days of Yom Kippur will never be nullified, as it says, "This will be for you an eternal statute [*Vayikra* 16:34]."[23]

It is apparent from the *Midrash* that, with the exception of Purim and *Yom HaKippurim*, all of the holidays, even those ordained by the Torah, will be nullified in the Messianic future. How is it possible that the holidays of the Torah will be canceled – is the Torah not eternal?! Did not *Rambam* himself teach us in this *halacha* that in the Messianic future the Torah itself would not be nullified?

R. Shlomo Halevi Alkabetz explains that the term "nullification" does not mean that we will stop celebrating the holidays altogether and that they will cease to exist. Rather, the significance of our holidays will pale in the great light that will appear in the Messianic era. The light of the present holidays compared to the Messianic light will be like a candle in the noon sunshine – a tiny, insignificant glow. The significance of our present lives will pale in comparison with the great light of life in the Messianic future.

Kippurim and Purim which exist forever

We have explained the matter of the nullification of the holidays in the Messianic future. Now we must understand the special quality of those holidays that will *not* be nullified.

Aside from establishing that all of the holidays will be nullified except for Purim, the aforementioned *midrash* adds that "likewise, the days of *Kippurim* will never be nullified." This incredible comparison between Purim and *Kippurim* has its source in the *Tikkunei Zohar*: "Purim is named after *Kippurim*, for in the future it will be a day of delight, transformed from suffering to pleasure."[24] It is well known that the name "*Kippurim*" can be understood to mean "like Purim" – as if to say that Yom Kippur is similar to Purim, but not on as high a level.[25] The idea that Purim is on a higher level than Yom Kippur is difficult to comprehend!

The *Shelah HaKadosh* explains that Yom Kippur represents the nullification of the material aspect of mankind. During the other days of the year, the relentless demands of the body oppress us. Our unceasing physical needs prevent us from focusing on spiritual elevation. Yom Kippur is the one day of the year, "the day of rest of the Tenth," the "Sabbath of Sabbaths," when we allow our body to come to rest. By means of the five bodily afflictions that we accept upon ourselves,[26] we become liberated from the body and we rid ourselves of the powers that oppress us. We become like angels, reciting in a loud voice at the end of Yom Kippur, "Blessed be the name of His glorious kingdom forever."

Purim, in contrast, is not a day when we suppress and disregard the needs of our body, but rather a time when we elevate the body to a state of holiness. This is the highest ideal – not suppression, but transformation. The verse in the *Megilla*, "It was transformed, for the Jews prevailed over their enemies,"[27] can be understood to refer to both external and internal opponents. On Purim, we achieve the transformation of our internal enemy, the harmful forces of physicality which hinder our spiritual progress. On Yom Kippur, we stifle the body in order to enable spiritual elevation, but the transformation effected on Purim is considered a more superior accomplishment.[28] In summary, the allusion to Purim in the name "*Kippurim*" suggests that Yom Kippur is like Purim in that it liberates the person from the chains of his material needs; it stands, however, on a lower plane.

The *Mitzva* to Drink

Revelation of the hidden nature of Am Yisrael

The nature of Purim is expressed in an extraordinary *halacha*: "A person is required to become so intoxicated on Purim that he no longer knows the difference between 'cursed be Haman' and 'blessed be Mordechai.'"[29] The medieval commentators have already expressed their astonishment. How can there be a *mitzva* obliging one to get drunk on Purim?[30] Isn't a drunkard akin to one who practices idolatry,[31] and isn't the prayer of one who prays while drunk considered an abomination?[32]

R. Avraham Yitzchak Kook explains the concept of drunkenness on Purim: When a person gets drunk, the intellect departs and the more fundamental inclinations are revealed, as our Sages said, "When wine comes in, the secret goes out."[33] The Sages further said, "A man is known by his cup."[34] Concerning this, R. Kook commented, "Not only is a man known by his cup, but his whole nation is known as well."[35] The fundamental nature of the nation is revealed; the difference between *Am Yisrael* and the nations of the world is exposed through the drinking of wine. The Talmud describes what happened when, at the banquet that Achashverosh held for his ministers and subjects, they began to become inebriated:

The nations of the world that eat and drink always initiate irreverent and crude behavior. And so, at the banquet of that evil one, some said that Medean women were the most beautiful and some said that Persian women were the most beautiful. Achashverosh said to them, "The 'vessel' I use is neither Medean nor Persian, but rather Casdean. Would you like to see her?" They replied, "Yes, but only if she is naked."[36]

We see from this that what most preoccupies the minds of the nations of the world is female beauty! The government ministers and leaders of the business community who were present at the banquet all appeared to be dignified people, serious and well mannered. Yet, after a few drinks, their true essence emerged. Their public behavior may be admirable and we can definitely learn from their example. In fact, the Talmud praises some elements of modesty found among the Persians.[37] But this is simply a veneer. Inside, they are morally bankrupt.

In contrast, when *Am Yisrael* drinks, the inner core of the nation is exposed: complete holiness, sweetness and refinement. The liquor reveals that we are a holy species, for when we become drunk, we can increase our piety and devotion to God.[38] Collectively, we are on the level of, "He that becomes soothed by his wine possesses one of the attributes of his Creator."[39] One may argue, perhaps, that we should drink wine every day of the year in order to reveal our internal commitment to God. The answer to this is: No, this is not the case, for the day of Purim has a special inherent power to restrain us. On this day of Purim, a holy elevation takes place and one's body becomes sanctified.[40] Each festival has its unique spiritual influence: for example, the spirit of freedom prevails on Pesach, and the spirit of repentance illuminates the days of Judgment.[41]

On Purim we willingly received that Torah which at Sinai we had received through coercion.[42] The terrible threat to the fate of *Am Yisrael*, the terror at the annihilation that could have happened, and the miracle of the salvation which then occurred – all of these aroused our love for the Torah. We matured. Our special inner nature began to shine within us. We strongly identified with the Torah and with the Master of the World.

Every year on Purim, when we relive those high moments of spiritual acceptance, the same inner power returns and is revealed. We therefore drink wine, for in the exceptional spiritual character of the day, there is an enhanced capacity for exercising caution, and through the wine, our internal purity can be revealed. Therefore, "the days of Purim will never pass from the Jews and their memory will not cease from their descendants," for these days mark the appearance of the uniquely holy capacity of *Am Yisrael*.

The Aramaic word used by our Sages to express the obligation to drink on Purim is "*levesumei*." This word is not the most common term for getting drunk, but rather it has the connotation of "to become fragrant." Our Sages state that "when the Torah was given, the world was filled with fragrance at every Divine utterance."[43] The Torah is a sweet perfume[44] that emerges from the inner character of the Jew, which is also a sweet aroma. It can be said that the Torah is our inner nature. The fundamental value of *Am Yisrael* is not dependent on our behavior, on whether or not we actually observe the Torah. In other words, our claim to the Torah does not begin with our own efforts, but rather it is part of our essence, our very nature. The Talmud relates the story of a non-Jew who attempted to provoke R. Chanina by saying, "You Jews are impure, as it says, 'Her impurity is on the hems of her skirts.'"[45] R. Chanina answered him, "God dwells with them amidst their impurity."[46] Even when *Am Yisrael* is impure, the Divine presence is among them.[47] Even when our behavior is improper, we remain the children of God.[48] We are still connected to God and Torah in our very essence.

At times we become alienated from Torah, our heart and core; on Purim this link is restored. *Rashba* expands on this concept by connecting it to the idea of the ultimate nullification of the festivals, with the exception of Purim. God did not promise that the other holidays would exist forever, for perhaps our sins would make us unworthy to have them, as the prophet says, "God caused the Shabbat and festivals to be forgotten in Zion."[49] But regarding Purim, God has promised that it will not be forgotten. And similarly, with regard to *Yom HaKippurim* it is written, "This will be for you as an eternal statute." This is a Divine promise that Yom Kippur will always effect atonement, even if we are not worthy and do not repent from our sins.[50] *Yom HaKippurim* does not atone as a result of our actions; rather, the powerful essence of the day itself effects atonement. This is possible because of the nature of *Am Yisrael*, which is unchanging and eternal in its attachment to God and therefore perpetually worthy of atonement. Likewise, the power of Purim stems from the inner eternal nature of *Am Yisrael*, and therefore Purim will never be nullified.[51] The famous poem recited on Purim, *Shoshanat Yaakov*, states, "Their salvation is forever" – the salvation of Purim will last forever. "The Eternal God of Israel will neither lie nor change His mind," because He made a promise to *Am Yisrael*, even if they sin.[52]

The historical process of clarification of the eternity of Am Yisrael

Purim clarifies and illuminates the eternal nature of the existence of *Am Yisrael*. Where can one find a more complex and confounding situation – was there ever a greater catastrophe than that of Purim? We were to be completely annihilated in one day![53] This was a threat more frightening than the Holocaust. Yet out of that fear and darkness, God shone for us, "in our lowliness He remembered us...and He redeemed us from our tormentors."[54] A great and historic revelation took place, showing that God does not abandon His nation, even in the most complicated and threatening of situations. Divine salvation from situations of darkness such as these emphasizes the eternity of *Am Yisrael*.

The assertion of our Sages that, "Greater is *kiddush Hashem* (the sanctification of God's name) than *chillul Hashem* (the desecration of God's name),"[55] can be restated as, "Greater is *kiddush Hashem* when it comes from *chillul Hashem*."[56] The events of the Purim story are the height of *chillul Hashem* because *Am Yisrael*, which is the heart of humanity and the hope of all worlds, faced complete annihilation due to Haman's decree. And then suddenly, everything was completely altered and reversed: "It was transformed, for the Jews prevailed over their enemies."[57] The physical eternity of *Am Yisrael* was revealed for all to see, as was their spiritual eternity, for they reaccepted the Torah with free will and desire. When *Am Yisrael* drinks and "becomes fragrant" on Purim, words of Torah flow out of our mouths, for the Torah is our inner essence. For this reason, Purim and *Megillat Esther* will not be nullified in the Messianic future, when all of the great miracles of the future Redemption will occur. This is because the days of Purim are the clearest possible revelation of the eternity of *Am Yisrael*. This eternity of our nation is the inner foundation and basis of all past and future redemptions.

The Messianic transformation

Purim is a Messianic holiday since it has within it the power of transformation, and this is the power of *Mashiach*. Our Sages relate that there are two *yeshivot* in heaven, and at the head of all of them is the *yeshiva* of the *Mashiach*. Not everyone can enter this *yeshiva*, for there is a prerequisite for admission: "He who does not know how to transform darkness to light and bitterness to sweetness must not enter here."[58] One who doesn't have the capacity to transform the depths of darkness to the greatness of light cannot be associated with the *yeshiva* of the *Mashiach*.

Purim is the holiday of transformation – "It was transformed, for the Jews prevailed over their enemies" – and it is therefore considered Messianic and unalterably associated with the future. On Purim, we are elevated by our drinking until we "cannot distinguish between 'cursed be Haman' and 'blessed be Mordechai.'" That is to say, we cannot distinguish between the cursed and the blessed, for the cursed is transformed into the blessed.[59] The *gematria* of Haman is the same as the term *chelbena*. *Chelbena* is one of the eleven spices used to make incense in the *Beit HaMikdash*. This spice has a foul odor on its own, but when it is joined with the other ten spices, it becomes pleasantly fragrant.[60] So, too, "cursed be Haman" – the very depth of accursed evil – is transformed into "blessed be Mordechai," the power of blessed righteousness. The power of Purim is the power of complete transformation; it is the power of the eternity of *Am Yisrael* that will never be nullified, and in the Messianic era, it will radiate with all its strength.

Lesson of Purim
Kneeling Saps Our Strength

W E CELEBRATE PURIM with great merriment because we all know the happy ending, but to the Jews of the time, their situation was terrifying: they were facing complete annihilation. In *Megillat Esther*, it seems as if Mordechai is to blame for endangering the entire *Am Yisrael* by not bowing down to Haman: "Mordechai would neither bow down nor prostrate himself [before Haman]."[61] At the time, it seemed to the Jews that Mordechai's refusal to bow down to Haman was the direct cause of his plan "to destroy, to kill, to annihilate all of the Jews, young and old, little children and women, in one day." However, their condemnation of Mordechai seems unjustified, because we know that we are prohibited from bowing down to idols. According to our Sages, Haman either engraved the image of an idol on his dress or attributed to himself the powers of a god.[62] It is well known that in those days, rulers were idolized, and that *Halacha* commands us to die rather than transgress in such a case.

Our Sages record how the Jews perceived the matter: "They said to Mordechai, 'Know that you are putting us at the mercy of that evil man's sword!'"[63] In *Megillat Esther* we read that the king's servants "spoke to [Mordechai] day after day saying, 'Why are you violating the king's law?' And he refused to listen to them.'"[64] A close reading of the *Megilla* reveals that Mordechai's actions were deliberate, even provocative. His refusal was no one-time act; he would go out of his way to pass near Haman in order to antagonize him! Had he wished, Mordechai could have avoided Haman. What is the explanation for such confrontational, dangerous behavior? Even when Mordechai saw that "Haman was filled with anger,"[65] he continued to provoke him. Thank God a miracle occurred and the Jews were saved, but it is well known that we are forbidden to rely on miracles.[66] We can't go around provoking our enemies in the hope that God will have mercy on us and extricate us from the situation. How can we understand Mordechai's behavior?

Descendant of Binyamin, born in Eretz Yisrael

The Talmud discusses the issue of what our strategy should be when dealing with our enemies. Should we try to placate them or provoke them? R. Shimon bar Yochai says that it is permitted to antagonize and provoke the wicked. He himself had to hide in a cave after he stood up to the Romans.[67] *Maharal* explains that challenging our enemies ultimately leads to a sanctification of God's name. However, the Talmud concludes that not every person in a dangerous situation should dare to act this way. Only a completely righteous person who has no ulterior motives can allow himself to take such a risk.

The *Midrash* recounts that Mordechai explained to Haman that the reason he would not bow down before him was that he was born of kings and was from the tribe of Binyamin, who was born in *Eretz Yisrael*, unlike all of Yaakov's other sons who were born in exile. Haman countered, "But Yaakov, Binyamin's father, bowed down before Eisav, my ancestor."[68] Mordechai answered in turn, "Yes, but that was before my ancestor, Binyamin, was born. He was born in *Eretz Yisrael*, and his soul, therefore, was an elevated soul. He would not bow down before others."[69] In fact, Yaakov was criticized for bowing down to Eisav, and *Ramban* goes so far as to say that this type of behavior led to trouble during the end of the period of the Hasmoneans.[70]

Kneeling saps our strength!

The philosophy of Mordechai was that there is no need to grovel or act in a subservient manner; instead, the Jews should stand together, proud and strong. The Jews, however, felt that in order to be able to achieve this strength, they needed to be strong themselves! How can one appear to be resolute without feeling inner strength? Mordechai's answer was: Who says we do not have strength? We do! The strength does not come from getting down on our knees; rather, the act of getting down on our knees leads us to mistakenly think that we that we don't possess the strength.

It is important for us to know that we have the strength. We need to develop an awareness of our latent abilities and powers. The fact is that the Jews succeeded in overcoming Haman. When the day came "that the Jews' enemies had hoped to rule over them, it was transformed, for the Jews prevailed over their enemies." The actual decree to kill the Jews had not been repealed; they were still required to take up arms against their enemies. At this point the Jews realized their strengths, understood their power, and took the initiative. This was in the merit of Mordechai who said to them: "Do you think that if we grovel before Haman, our problems will be solved? He is simply looking for excuses to destroy and annihilate the Jews. Today he demands that you bow down; tomorrow and the day after that will lead to demands for your annihilation. If you give in to evil, you are only inviting more evil." To all generations of Jews, the message is clear: We must be strong and proud and not capitulate out of weakness and lack of self-confidence.

The bear's "just" solution

I once heard a story during the disarmament talks between the United States and the Soviet Union. The American Secretary of Defense was asked if he trusted the Russians. The Secretary said, "I'll give you a parable. Once there was a hunter who saw a bear, and he aimed his gun to shoot at it. The bear said, 'Hey, what are you doing?' The hunter said, 'I need a fur and so I must kill you.' Said the bear, 'What do you know? I was just about to kill you, as I have not had a good meal in three days. I see that we both have legitimate demands. Let us sit and discuss our needs together, without preconditions, in order that we can reach a just and permanent solution which will take into account our mutual requirements.' The hunter felt that this was reasonable, and accompanied the bear to a cave to discuss the issues at hand. After a short while, the bear came out, alone and satiated. He explained, 'We have reached a permanent solution, even if not completely just. I have had my meal, and he is enveloped in my fur.'"

Mordechai teaches us that it is not through cowering that we can achieve long-sought-after peace and tranquility, but only though strength, pride and unequivocal firmness.

Pesach

How to Do Your Pesach Cleaning Happily
A Halachic Guide

Bedikat chametz

One need only search for *chametz* in places where there is a reasonable chance of finding it. All parents are familiar with their children's habits. Crumbs in the corners of the house do not constitute a *kezayit*; moreover, they are inedible to a dog. If there is bread hidden behind a cabinet in such a way that it is inaccessible, chances are that no one will be able to reach it on Pesach either, and it is considered buried. Similarly, you are not required to search under stones or under the house's foundations, since nobody will take *chametz* from there.

It is a good idea to start *bedikat chametz* in a place where *chametz* was actually eaten, so that the *beracha* is relevant.

Chametz smaller than a kezayit

Rooms into which *chametz* is not normally brought need not be thoroughly cleaned, as the chance of finding a piece of *chametz* the size of a *kezayit* (three centimeters, or a little over one inch, square) is negligible. It is certainly forbidden to *eat* any *chametz* at all on Pesach, but if it is smaller than this size, it is not included in the Torah prohibition of "*bal yeira'eh*,"[1] – the prohibition of having it in the house – especially if one has sold his *chametz*.[2] Generally, pieces of *chametz* the size of a *kezayit* are only found in those rooms in which children are allowed to eat sandwiches or cookies.

Incidentally, for *bedikat chametz*, one must take care not to hide pieces

99

of *chametz* which are the size of a *kezayit* or larger, in case one of the pieces should get lost. In the event that this does take place, you can rely on the *bitul chametz* (formula which declares renunciation of ownership of *chametz*) that you recite after the *bedika*.[3]

When one is away for Pesach

If you won't be at home for the duration of Pesach, you can rely on the lenient opinion which states that you need not do any Pesach cleaning at all. Simply close up all the rooms, seal them with tape and sell all of the *chametz* in the house.[4]

If, on Pesach, part of the house will be lived in, however, only that section must be cleaned. The question remains: How should a person in this situation fulfill the *mitzva* of *bedikat chametz*? If you leave your permanent home before the eve of *bedikat chametz* (14th of *Nisan*), you should perform the search wherever you are that evening. If you will still be at home until the next morning (15th of *Nisan*), you should clean the smallest room and remove from it any *chametz*. After that, you must perform, in the rooms in which you *will* stay during Pesach, the *bedika* with a *beracha* – if it hasn't previously been done for you.

Children's clothes and toys

Chametz may be found in your children's pockets, for a child may have put a hand into his or her pocket while eating. Still, it is unnecessary to check any clothes that will not be worn during Pesach. Simply lock them in a cupboard. Since running clothes through the washing machine will not necessarily remove all the crumbs, clothes that will be worn on Pesach must be checked.

The best way to deal with your children's toy collection is to put some, or all, of the toys and games away (seal them in plastic bags) and buy new ones for the holiday! That will serve the double purpose of saving yourself work and making your children happy. Remember: On Pesach there isn't very much time for playing – there are days of *Yom Tov*, and on *Chol HaMoed* many families go away on trips. While cleaning, you often end up sorting and arranging as well, which can be an endless task.

Toys that will be played with on Pesach must be checked. You can simply immerse plastic toys in strong detergent. Often, children have a favorite toy, so you can clean just that particular one.

Bathroom cabinets

There are many different kinds of creams, toothpaste, toiletries and medicines which may contain *chametz*, such as wheat germ oil and alcohol derived from wheat. There is no need to clean the cabinets: simply seal them, sell the *chametz*, and buy products that are kosher for Pesach.

Furniture

Sofas and chairs: Clean in all the crevices and between the pillows. This is a great opportunity to find all sorts of lost possessions.

High chair: If it is plastic, it should be soaked in a tub with boiling water and cleaning agents for two to three hours. It is unnecessary to dismantle it, because whatever is in the cracks and holes is inedible, even to a dog. Clean the crevices with a stiff brush.

Books

It is nearly impossible for a *kezayit* of *chametz* to be hidden inside a book! If there is a possibility that a book has *chametz* inside it, it must be thoroughly checked. It is not sufficient to place books on the porch so that the wind will turn the pages. However, most books do not need to be cleaned or checked. It is sufficient to clean and check the few books that you'll want to read at the table on Pesach. It is customary, during Pesach, not to place on the table books which have not been checked for *chametz*.

Dining room

One need only clean in the actual eating areas. Chairs should be wiped clean if they are dirty. If you are intending to use the table during Pesach, it should be *kashered* by pouring boiling water on it. Since people don't generally place boiling pots on the table, there is no need to use water from a boiling kettle that is still plugged in. Alternatively, it may be covered with several layers of plastic and cloth tablecloths.

Kitchen

The kitchen must be thoroughly cleaned of every crumb of *chametz*. A crumb of *chametz* isn't considered nullified – and isn't permitted to be eaten – even when diluted in a food one thousand times its volume.

Dishwasher: It is preferable not to *kasher* a dishwasher; it contains many rubber parts and connections and thus requires a lot of hard work. Dishes can be washed by hand, as was the practice in all previous generations. If necessary, use disposable cutlery and crockery.

Oven: If you do not have a self-cleaning oven, it is best not to *kasher* it. Seal the oven and buy baked goods or, alternatively, bake with a wonder-pot on top of the stove.

Stove: In order to save time and energy, it is a good idea to purchase special Pesach grids. If this is not an option, cover the grids with aluminum foil that is thick enough not to tear, but thin enough to bend and shape. The control knobs should be wiped clean with a rag. There is no need to clean the burners; any food in or on them will, in any event, be destroyed by fire in the course of use. The surface of the stove is considered nonkosher year-round and food that spills on it is discarded. Therefore, it is sufficient to cover it with aluminum foil.

Refrigerator and freezer: These must be defrosted and thoroughly cleaned including the doors' rubber parts. It is best to finish eating the *chametz* that is stored in them before Pesach, but if expensive food which contains *chametz* is left over, it may be wrapped well in several layers, sealed, clearly labeled "*Chametz*," stored in the back of the freezer/refrigerator and included in the list of *chametz* sold before Pesach. If you have an old refrigerator with cracks and crevices that prove difficult to clean, you should line the shelves and door with plastic.

Microwave oven: To *kasher* a microwave, don't use it for 24 hours, clean it thoroughly, and boil water in it for half an hour. All food cooked or baked in it on Pesach should be placed in a covered dish, but it doesn't have to be hermetically sealed.

Toaster: A toaster cannot be properly cleaned or *kashered*. It should be put away with the *chametz* that is sold.

Food processor: If you want to use your mixer, blender or food processor on Pesach, the body has to be thoroughly cleaned and wrapped in plastic, leaving air holes open. Beaters and bowls must be *kashered* by immersing them in boiling water, or should be replaced. It is preferable, though, to buy a small, cheap hand mixer for use on Pesach.

Counters: There are two options:

1 You can cover the counters with heavy-duty aluminum foil after wiping them clean. Because the counters are covered, there is no need to *kasher* them.

2 The counters can be *kashered* by thoroughly cleaning the crevices with bleach and then pouring boiling water over them from an electric kettle that is still boiling. This is best achieved by two people working together.

Sink: There are three options:

1 On Pesach don't put anything into the sink; simply wash the dishes in the air. This, however, is unrealistic.

2 Put a plastic bowl inside the sink, making sure there is still a direct flow down the drain.

3 Clean and *kasher* in the same way as the counters.

Kitchen cabinets: Shelves and drawers that will not be used on Pesach may be sealed and need not be cleaned. There are some people who prefer to be strict and wash even their *chametzdik* dishes. But there are three reasons for leniency, each of which alone would be sufficient:

1 We sell all the crumbs together with the sale of *chametz*.

2 The dishes are clean. Nobody puts a dirty dish away in a cupboard.

3 Even if *chametzdik* dirt can be found, it will definitely be less than a *kezayit*.

Cutlery and crockery: *Kashering* dishes, pots and utensils requires a tremendous amount of work. It is preferable to buy new dishes. True, it is expensive, so try accumulating a collection gradually, buying a few new things each year. As for pots, it's possible to buy cheap aluminum ones. It's true that doctors are wary of aluminum, but these pots will only be used for seven days. You can buy cheap plastic plates, cutlery and foil containers.

Cars

Cars must be thoroughly cleaned, including all compartments and under the mats. Take out the mats and gather the *chametzdik* dirt by hand; there is no need for a vacuum cleaner. One need not use a lot of water or take the car apart. In general, it is not necessary to dismantle anything that requires the use of pliers. *Chametz* that can't be reached without turning the car (or house) upside down will not be seen or eaten on Pesach either.

Chumrot, or stringencies

If you know that in your Pesach cleaning you are being stricter than *Halacha* requires – and you make an informed choice to be so strict – you are to be commended. However, if the *chumra* you accepted upon yourself becomes too hard to continue, you may perform *hatarat nedarim*, which is the process of annulling a vow. If you were under the impression that the *chumra* you were performing was required by *Halacha*, and now you realize that it was actually a *chumra*, you need not do *hatarat nedarim*. In general, we should not take stringencies upon ourselves unless we can perform them with love and are willing to invest the energy and effort they require. Regarding Pesach, in particular, all who take on a *chumra* in the correct way deserve to be blessed.

Summary

In light of what is written above, it shouldn't take more than a day to clean the entire house, including the kitchen. Anything more than that is a stringency. If we take on an extra workload which we are not capable of dealing with, we deplete our energy and take out our exhaustion on our families. Not only is there increased tension between husband and wife as a result, but we set our children a very negative example. It is all too easy, in the heat of the moment to shout at your children: "I told you not to go into this room anymore. Why did you go in?!" "Eat on the porch!" "Eat standing up!" "Don't touch!"

The whole kitchen will look like it was overturned by vandals – the husband and children will tremble in fear, eating in some corner, while the woman of the house glares at them like a drill sergeant. Is this preparation for Pesach?! Is this educating children?! No, it is a reign of terror with the mother presiding as Pharaoh.

Our goal should be to involve the whole family in Pesach cleaning and make it a happy, exciting experience. We should set our priorities before we begin, and finish cleaning that which is necessary in the kitchen and dining room before we set out to spring-clean the rest of the house.

The *Shulchan Aruch* writes: "Every person should sweep his room before *bedikat chametz*, and check his pockets for *chametz*."[5] The *Mishna Berura* adds: "It is the custom to sweep the whole house on the thirteenth of *Nisan*, so that it will be ready for *bedikat chametz* immediately after nightfall on the fourteenth." Anything more than that is a *chumra*, and should not come at the cost of health and happiness and at the expense of one's husband and children.

Most of the practical suggestions that I have heard regarding how to reduce the burden of cleaning come from women themselves. Even if you do more than I have outlined here, the very knowledge that what one is undertaking is a *chumra* reduces the stress involved. Even a woman who has a strong desire to clean as much as she can, and finds joy in it, will benefit from what has been said above, because she will not feel pressured that she might violate *Halacha*, but, instead, will proceed with satisfaction and peace of mind.

The main point is the distinction between *chametz* – which there is a strict halachic obligation to clean and remove – and dirt, which one should make a point of removing, but not necessarily before Pesach. Not all dirt is *chametz*. Stand before *chametz* with awe and fear; but when cleaning for Pesach, don't approach dirt in the same frame of mind. You can spread the work out over the whole year so that your families will not suffer before Pesach.

If your children are on vacation before Pesach, it is preferable to spend this time playing with them, preparing for the *seder*, taking family trips, etc. Spring-cleaning can be done some other time – preferably spread out over the whole year. We were freed from slavery when we left Egypt, and should not allow ourselves to be so fatigued that we are unable to enjoy the *seder* and the Pesach holiday. After all, the month of *Nisan* is meant to be a month of joy. We were not freed from bondage in Egypt in order to recreate our own slavery! A woman should make sure she has allocated herself some free time to spend with her husband and children without feeling harried and pressured by Pesach cleaning.

Obviously, I am not objecting to a thorough cleaning of one's house. But I recommend spacing it out over the course of the year: clean a different room every few months, or tackle some other household project. The week before Pesach is not the time for undertaking extra housework. It's next to impossible to arrive at *seder* night having created a perfectly orderly and spotless home. We should, instead, strive to approach the *seder* in a relaxed frame of mind, ready to provide an uplifting experience for the whole family.

The answer to the question of whether a husband is obligated to help his wife with the Pesach cleaning is that a husband does not have to help his wife, nor a wife her husband. Rather, the two of them together have to clean, since this is a shared home, and likewise a shared life. If a husband is on vacation from work, this may be a good time to leave him with the children and give his wife a vacation! Regardless, our first priority must be to try to make the *seder* an unforgettable, inspiring experience for all.

We wish you all a happy and kosher Pesach. See to it that you come to *seder* night rested and happy, so that the night will inspire you and your children with faith in God, the Redeemer of Israel.

Shabbat HaGadol – The Great Day

THE SHABBAT BEFORE PESACH is called *Shabbat HaGadol* – The Great Shabbat. The real meaning of this term is the subject of much discussion by rabbinic commentators. The most famous interpretation – offered by *Rashi* and Tosafot – is that this day marked the beginning of the miracles of redemption. This is when *Bnei Yisrael* broke free of the evils of Egypt by setting aside a lamb for the Paschal offering on the tenth of *Nisan*, which fell on Shabbat. The Egyptians were ready to kill the Jews because sheep were held to be sacred in Egypt, but miraculously they were not harmed. Thus, according to this interpretation, *Shabbat HaGadol* is both the day when the miracles of the redemption began and the day when Jewish courage and valor were first demonstrated – and this convergence is not coincidental.

The Talmud asks why it is that in our times, as opposed to biblical times, miracles rarely occur. How are we different? Is it because we don't study enough Torah? No, answers the Talmud. It can be proven that there were generations that studied less Torah than we do, but nonetheless experienced far greater miracles. The difference is that earlier generations risked their lives for the sanctification of the Divine name. Compared to them, we sacrifice very little. The Talmud goes on to relate the story of a sage from an earlier generation who followed the Torah with absolutely no reservations, despite the heavy price exacted. Thus, the connection between miracles and courage is clear – miracles are the result of valor and selfless devotion.[6]

Maharshal, in a different vein, explains that the name *Shabbat HaGadol* is derived from the last verse of the *haftara* reading for that day, "For behold I will send you the prophet Eliyahu before the arrival of the great (*gadol*) and awesome day of God."[7] What connection does *Shabbat HaGadol* have with this great and awesome day? *Shabbat HaGadol* was the last Shabbat of *Bnei Yisrael's* exile in Egypt as they awaited their redemption; the "great day" refers to the transition from exile to Redemption. This verse appears at the end of the book of *Malachi* – the last prophet – the one who bridges the period between clearly perceived Divine revelation and exile. It is the last verse of the last prophet which announces the onset of the first sparks of light and Redemption. This Great Day marks the transition between the two periods, a kind of dawn between night and day.

In our times, we, too are living in a "Great Day" – the *Shabbat HaGadol* before the final Redemption. We know this from three faithful witnesses:

1 The *Midrash*: "Three days before the *Mashiach* is to come, Eliyahu will come and stand upon the mountains of *Eretz Yisrael* and cry and mourn over them saying, 'Mountains of *Eretz Yisrael*, how long will you remain dry and desolate?' And his voice will be heard from one end of the world to the other. Then he will say to them, 'Peace has come forever.'"[8]

Happy is the generation who heeded the voice of Eliyahu and came to make the deserts and mountains bloom and thus bring peace. R. Avraham Yitzchak Kook wrote in a similar vein about the "awakening of the desire of the nation to return to its Land, to its essence," referring to the awakening of repentance which is part of our redemptive process.

2 *Ravad* wrote that the day before the *Mashiach* comes, Eliyahu the prophet will appear "to bring about peace for Israel with the nations of the world, and to announce the coming of the *Mashiach*, as it is written, 'For behold I send you the prophet Eliyahu before the arrival of the great and awesome day of God, and he shall return the hearts of fathers to their sons and the hearts of sons to their fathers.' This means that the hearts of the fathers and sons had been overcome with fear and each had run in a different direction from their troubles. On that day, they will return to their former state of valor; they will turn to each other and be comforted by each other. May it happen in our generation."[9]

Thus we see that before the *Mashiach* arrives, courage returns to our people – which actually brings us peace with the other nations.

3 R. Zadok HaKohen of Lublin explains that: "Eliyahu…coming before the time of the *Mashiach*, means that his strength will make itself felt in the hearts of *Am Yisrael*…to be able to use the traits of anger and revenge against the idolaters. The coming of Eliyahu is really the arising of a strong arm, which will result in the awakening in their hearts…."[10]

Happy are we who are privileged to live during this great hour, as our Redemption approaches and gathers daily momentum, through the wonders which God, the Lord and Redeemer of Israel, has performed for His people and His inheritance.

Commentary on the *Haggada*
Ma'aseh BeRabbi Eliezer

מעשה ברבי אליעזר ורבי יהושע ורבי אלעזר בן עזריה ורבי עקיבא ורבי טרפון,
שהיו מסובין בבני ברק, והיו מספרים ביציאת מצרים כל אותו הלילה, עד שבאו
תלמידיהם ואמרו להם: רבותינו, הגיע זמן קריאת שמע של שחרית.

It once happened that Rabbi Eliezer, Rabbi Joshua, Rabbi Elazar ben Azarya,
Rabbi Akiva and Rabbi Tarfon were celebrating the *seder* together in Bnei
Brak. They spent the whole night telling about the Exodus from Egypt.
Finally, their students came and said to them, "Rabbis, it is time to say the
Shema of the morning service."

R. Judah Leib Maimon (a leader of the Mizrachi movement fifty years ago)
analyzed this passage of the *Haggada* from a political-historical perspective.
Bnei Brak was R. Akiva's hometown; all the other sages lived elsewhere. R.
Yehoshua, for example, lived in Peki'in, and R. Eliezer in Lod.[11] Why did
these four great rabbis come to Bnei Brak to hold a *seder*, instead of being
at home with their families?

R. Maimon suggests that this *seder* in Bnei Brak was really a guise for a
secret political and military conference. That is why they came to R. Akiva,
who was both a venerated sage and a military expert. He was Bar Kochba's
right-hand man, so to speak,[12] and the spiritual force behind the Bar Kochba
Revolt against the Roman Legions. Thus, the rabbinic leaders of his time
took the exceptional step of coming to him for the *seder* in order to hold a

strategic summit there.[13] R. Akiva declared Bar Kochba to be the *Mashiach* and cited the verse, "A star (*kochav*) shall shoot out from Yaakov," as a prediction of his leadership.[14]

With the unfolding of history, we know that Bar Kochba was proven not to be the *Mashiach*. So how do we understand a sage of R. Akiva's caliber supporting him in this way? Wasn't this a serious misjudgment? Heaven forbid! A giant such as R. Akiva does not err. Even at the time, no one dared publicly disagree with R. Akiva (except for one sage who told him, "Grass will grow out of your cheeks before the [*Mashiach*] Son of David comes!"[15])

There were, however, some who had certain reservations. They felt that Bar Kochba did not fit the prophet Yeshayahu's description of the *Mashiach*: "The spirit of God shall rest upon him, a spirit of wisdom and understanding, a spirit of counsel and courage, a spirit of knowledge and fear of God, and he shall find delight in the fear of God."[16] R. Akiva, however, did not let this deter him.[17] He regarded Bar Kochba's proud Jewish identity, his heroism and his courage – which enabled him to conquer the Romans, bringing salvation and independence to *Eretz Yisrael* for several years – as the deciding factors.[18] Our Sages have never stated that R. Akiva erred in this. Even *Rambam* does not state that he made a mistake by *encouraging* Bar Kochba, but that "he and all the Sages of his generation [erred when they] *imagined* that he was the *Mashiach*."[19] R. Akiva interpreted Bar Kochba's leadership and valor as Messianic, though it turned out to be false.[20]

In 1934, shortly before he passed away, R. Avraham Yitzchak Kook wrote a letter to the newly founded Bnei Akiva youth movement, which took R. Akiva as its role model:

> As the Redemption blossoms, that special quality of R. Akiva is returning to *Am Yisrael* – that enthusiasm for, and devotion to, the vision of Redemption and rejuvenation of the nation and of *Eretz Yisrael*.[21] It is coming back to life to guide us once again today. It is precisely because that vision originally failed, and Bar Kochba lost the war and *Eretz Yisrael* its independence, that we are confident that R. Akiva's vision will one day come true. It was not for nothing that *Am Yisrael* has been fighting for its existence throughout all generations. We shall not fail the second time. Eventually we shall be victorious. That hour is fast approaching.[22]

The process of Redemption and renewal today is simply a modern version of the Bar Kochba Revolt. Our own revolution – the 1948 War of Independence – was, with God's mercy, successful. The nation is reawakening, and this time we shall be redeemed, with the help of God.

The Ten Plagues

It is no coincidence that there were exactly ten plagues, as it says in *Sefer Yetzira*, "Ten and not nine, ten and not eleven."[23] What is the significance of the number ten? It signifies a whole unit, including within it all of the individual parts, as well as all of the possible variations on a theme. The number ten is used in many different instances in the Torah to reflect this idea:

- "The world was created with *ten* sayings," which embody all the inherent possibilities of Divine revelation in each creation.
- "There were *ten* generations between Adam and Noach," which include within them every possible portrayal of the species of mankind.
- "Avraham was tested with *ten* tests," each of which revealed another aspect of his unique personality and brought to the fore his diverse spiritual strengths.
- "Our forefathers tested God with *ten* tests in the wilderness," which include within them every type of provocation which distances a Jew from the Divine light.

And here we have the same idea:

- "God smote the Egyptians with ten plagues," which include every form of attack on a nation which defied the idea of Divine providence in the world.[24]

The plagues did not all appear simultaneously as a sudden and immediate act. Rather, they took place gradually, over an extended period of time. The world was also created piece by piece with ten sayings, even though it could easily have been created with just one. From the perspective of Divine power, there was nothing to prevent the world from being created with one utterance. But there is a universal human inability to absorb a creation of that sort on a cognitive, emotional and practical level. Abrupt changes can sometimes breed unendurable crises. For this reason, the plagues in Egypt did not come all at once. Nor did they begin with the most severe – the Plague of the Firstborn. Instead, step by step, the destruction of Egypt and the creation of *Am Yisrael* became increasingly apparent to Egyptians and Israelites alike. This psychological upheaval did not happen in a single day, or even in a month. Rather, Jewish and Egyptian hearts gradually absorbed this fundamental change in the course of world history.

It takes time to get used to a new manifestation of God in the world. As God rhetorically asks through Yeshayahu, "Can the earth be made to bring forth in one day; can a nation be conceived in a moment?"[25] The course of creation proceeds slowly but surely, as Yeshayahu continues, "Will I induce labor and not bring about birth? Will I, who brings about birth, then stop it?"[26] The fact that the process is gradual aids in human acceptance of the phenomenon. So, too, the development of *Am Yisrael* today is gradual, and does not come about through miraculous leaps: that is the way God redeems His people. Just as the process of childbirth has its stages – beginning slowly and progressing with ever-increasing labor pains – so it is with the birth of *Am Yisrael*.

Why the Pesach Sacrifice?

IN THE *Haggada*, we read the following well-known passage: "R. Gamliel would say: Whoever has not made mention of these three things on Pesach has not fulfilled his obligation [to remember the Exodus]: *Pesach, matza* and *maror*."²⁷ These three things, therefore, are the fundamentals of Pesach, and merely reciting them without understanding their essence is insufficient.

The *Haggada* continues by explaining the three things. The first one is Pesach:

> What is the reason for this Pesach [sacrifice], which our forefathers ate when the *Beit HaMikdash* was standing? It is because God "passed over" (*pasach*) our forefathers' houses in Egypt, as it is written: "And you shall declare – this is the Pesach sacrifice to God who passed over the houses of *Bnei Yisrael* in Egypt, when He smote the Egyptians but saved our houses [*Shemot* 12:27]."²⁸

We thus conclude that the Pesach sacrifice commemorates the "passing over" in Egypt.

This miracle is difficult to understand. God's passing over the houses seems to imply that He had originally intended to kill all Jewish firstborn children too! How could that be? Weren't all the plagues intended to *save* the Jews? How could anyone imagine that Jews would be killed in the last plague?

After 210 years of life in Egypt, the Jews had sunk into "forty-nine gates of impurity (*tuma*)," until it was almost impossible to differentiate between Egyptians and Jews. According to the Kabbalists, had *Bnei Yisrael* remained in Egypt any longer, they would have sunk into the fiftieth gate, and it would no longer have been possible to redeem them.[29]

This is exactly what Uzza, the angel of Egypt, protested in Heaven as the Red Sea was being split for the Jews while the Egyptians were drowning: "Both Egyptians and Jews are idol-worshipers…. Why do you discriminate by saving one nation and drowning the other?" Similarly, the prophet Yechezkel describes the grievous failure of *Bnei Yisrael*: "They rebelled against Me and did not agree to listen to Me; no man would cast off his idols, nor forsake the gods of Egypt. I thought to pour out My wrath upon them, to annihilate them in My anger in the land of Egypt."[30]

Thus, the miracle of passing over the Jewish houses teaches us a momentous lesson. God chose us not for our righteousness – as our deeds were also evil – but rather out of His love for us. In other words, He lovingly created a Jewish nation with an eternal Jewish soul, which not even debased behavior can extinguish. Passing over the Jewish houses, distinguishing between the Jewish and Egyptian firstborns – identical as they may have seemed in both appearance and behavior – is the greatest miracle of all, and the source of all other miracles which God in His mercy has performed for us.

This is why R. Gamliel, in his God-inspired wisdom, declared that one who has not made mention of the Pesach sacrifice has not fulfilled his obligation, for he has not understood the basic idea of the Exodus from Egypt.

The Splitting of the Sea

THE ADMOR OF GUR once asked: Why was the Splitting of the Sea considered such a great miracle for *Am Yisrael*? Wasn't the very same miracle performed for just a single individual – R. Pinchas ben Yair? The story of R. Pinchas ben Yair's miracle is related in the Talmud:

> One time on his way to redeeming captives, R. Pinchas came to a treacherous river called Ginai. R. Pinchas commanded, "Ginai, split so that I may pass through!" The river responded, "You are following your Master's commands and so am I. You, however, may not succeed, whereas I will always succeed in following His command." R. Pinchas said, "If you don't split, I will decree that no water flow here forever!" The river split.

Thus, the Talmud concludes, R. Pinchas ben Yair had the power of Moshe Rabbeinu and all 600,000 of *Am Yisrael* put together.[31]

R. Zadok HaKohen of Lublin points out that the Splitting of the Sea is, in the same way, a sign of the worth of *Am Yisrael*. The fact that God performs miracles for righteous individuals proves that the miracles performed for *Am Yisrael* – for example, the Splitting of the Sea – are a measure of the greatness of our nation.[32]

R. Zadok goes on to say that what looks like an exceptional miracle, when performed for an ordinary person, can happen every day to a man who is completely righteous (*tzaddik gamur*). In the Talmud, we are told that R. Chanina ben Dosa saw nothing unusual in instructing God: "He who commanded oil to burn can command vinegar to burn as well." He was poverty-stricken and had no oil to light the Shabbat candles; therefore, he used vinegar instead![33]

The biggest miracle of all is the revelation of the inner sanctity of *Am Yisrael* to all the nations of the world. Even though *Bnei Yisrael* were sunk in forty-nine gates of *tuma*, and, like the Egyptians, were idol worshipers, God nevertheless dwelt with them in the midst of all their uncleanliness and they, deep down, continued to cleave to God.

Our Sages tell us that, "A maidservant at the Red Sea had a greater vision than did the prophet Yechezkel ben Buzi [who saw the Heavens open]."[34] It was not the maidservant's own individual greatness which allowed her to see such a vision, but rather the fact that at that time the nation as a whole was on a sufficiently high level.[35] The Talmud goes on to relate that the waters split on behalf of individuals on two other occasions: once for a Jew who had the responsibility of guarding the Pesach *matza* from becoming *chametz*, and once for the Arab merchant who accompanied him. The waters did not only split for the *tzaddik*, R. Pinchas ben Yair, who was engaged in the great *mitzva* of redeeming captives; they split also for a simple Jew occupied with his own personal *mitzva*. R. Zvi Yehuda Kook explained that this was possible since every member of *Am Yisrael* has a share in the sanctity of the nation. Even a gentile accompanying them deserves to have the waters split for him.[36]

The Talmud continues with the story of R. Pinchas ben Yair's donkey, which refused to eat the barley offered to him at a hostel on the road. The barley was sifted to remove stones and dirt, but still she refused to touch it. Then R. Pinchas asked the hostel owner if *terumot* and *ma'asrot* (tithes) had been taken from the food. As soon as it was tithed, the donkey began to eat. R. Pinchas exclaimed: This poor animal only wishes to fulfill her Master's will, and you dare to feed her untithed barley! However, the Talmud asks, is there actually a requirement to tithe food which animals eat? In response, the commentary of *Tosafot* cites the *Talmud Yerushalmi*, which states that this donkey was being stricter than the letter of the law! R. Zvi Yehuda explains that we can see from this that anything connected to *Am Yisrael* – even if it is physical and material – falls within the realm of the miraculous because of the Divine sanctity of *Am Yisrael*. It is no coincidence that the animal mentioned here is a donkey. *Chamor* is Hebrew for donkey and *chomer* is the word for material matter, for things belonging in the physical realm.

The donkey, therefore, symbolizes the physical, material aspect of the world, which, when connected to sanctity, becomes elevated.

Thus, the miracle of the Splitting of the Sea for *Am Yisrael* expresses the idea that *Am Yisrael* as an entity is holy, with an inherent yearning for closeness to God.

Yom HaAtzmaut
The Birth of a Jewish State

The Process of Redemption

Fulfillment of the Divine promise of Redemption

The establishment of the State of Israel is not only a *mitzva*; it is also the fulfillment of the Divine promise of Redemption for *Am Yisrael*. In the Talmud, the sage Shmuel states: "There is no difference between our time and the Messianic period except that in that future time, *Am Yisrael* will be free from subservience to other nations."[1] *Rambam*, too, defines the Messianic period as one in which *Am Yisrael* is independent of any other nation.[2] It is clear that the establishment of an independent State of Israel is part of the Messianic process foretold by our prophets. Obviously, the establishment of the State is not the fulfillment of everything that our prophets promised; it is only one part of the Redemption.[3] However, the first step must be *Am Yisrael's* freedom from foreign rule. Only at a later stage will we achieve internal freedom, such that no Jew will be financially dependent on another. Thus, we see that the establishment of the State is both a *mitzva* which we are obligated to fulfill, and also God's fulfillment of His Divine promise to *Am Yisrael*.

The difference between a mitzva and a promise

There are many people who feel that there is a contradiction between a Divine promise and a *mitzva*: a Divine promise is God's to keep, while a *mitzva* is something we are obligated to fulfill. According to this view, God promised that we would one day be free from foreign rule, and we should therefore wait passively for it to happen. This is not so! The fact that God promised to redeem us does not exempt us from taking responsibility. His promise does not release us from the *mitzva* that we are obligated to fulfill. On the contrary, it obligates and motivates us to do everything in our power to actualize the promise. Had God not promised us that we would be independent, we might feel there was no point in making an effort to achieve it, because perhaps we would never reach that point. But since we know that God has promised us independence, we must do everything in our power to fulfill the *mitzva*, for we are certain that in the end we will succeed.

In a similar fashion, *Rambam* refers to the promise in the Torah that *Am Yisrael* will eventually do *teshuva*.[4] Should we conclude from that promise that we need not invest any effort in educating our fellow human being, or in improving ourselves, since we know that in the end everyone will do *teshuva* anyway? Obviously not. We must certainly try as hard as we can to elevate ourselves and others. The fact that the Torah has promised us that our efforts will succeed only serves to motivate us to try harder, even though we have no idea when this promise will be fulfilled. It may take hundreds, or even thousands, of years, but eventually it will happen. Therefore, we see that the Divine promise does not negate the need for our own input. On the contrary, it provides the motivation and impetus for our efforts.

This idea can be understood by the following parable: A famous musician tests a child and says, "That child is talented. He will certainly be a great musician when he grows up." This statement does not promise that one day the child will magically turn into a great musician without any effort. It simply means that the child has the ability to become a great musician if he develops his talents and works hard. No achievements are reached without effort; on the other hand, without the potential to succeed, no amount of hard work will help.

Thus, the establishment of the State of Israel is both a *mitzva* achieved through intensive labor and the fulfillment of a Divine promise. It is the result of a partnership between our Creator and His nation. His promise lays the foundation for our efforts. Without it, our endeavors would be in vain. But on the other hand, His promise can only be fulfilled through our exertions.

The Redemption is a process
The redemptive process, as we see it today, is a gradual one. God, if He so wills, can bring the Redemption in an instant, or He can bring it about little

by little. He does not owe us anything. He brought us out of Egypt in haste, but in the days of Ezra and Nechemia, He redeemed us slowly. Today, too, our Creator is returning His presence to Zion measure by measure.

The world itself was created through a process of ongoing development. On the first day, light was created. On each additional day, something new was added and the world developed, until finally, on the sixth day, mankind – the crown of Creation – was fashioned, and we are told that "it was very good."[5] Later, when Cain killed Hevel, it became apparent that mankind was not so very good. There were only two brothers in the whole world, and they lacked the ability to coexist peacefully.

We see that the history of mankind has also evolved gradually. Mankind has the potential to be "very good," but in actuality, this was not always the case. The ten generations from Adam to Noach grew ever more corrupt, until finally God brought a flood upon the world. Another ten generations of vice followed, from Noach to Avraham.[6] No less than twenty generations elapsed from Creation until the appearance of Avraham. Avraham, who was truly "very good," was the realization of the Divine potential of Creation, but God was not satisfied only with holy individuals. His goal was for there to be a holy nation, and Avraham was designated to pave the way for this objective.

God promised Avraham, "I shall make you into a great nation."[7] This was not accomplished in one day. Yitzchak clashed with Yishmael, Yaakov with Eisav, the twelve tribes descended to Egypt and suffered there for hundreds of years – until finally we became a nation. We left Egypt and wandered for years in the desert. The generation who left Egypt died in the desert and a new generation entered *Eretz Yisrael*. Did life then become utopian? Did we all live happily and peacefully as a holy nation in our own Land? No! It took hundreds of years of fighting one another, and fighting wars against the Canaanites and Philistines, and of Jews committing sins of idolatry, adultery and bloodshed, until we finally reached the golden age of David and Shlomo. And then we stumbled again.

During the second period of redemption, in the days of the Return to Zion of Ezra and Nechemia, there were also many crises. Hate and deception delayed the building of the *Beit HaMikdash*; our non-Jewish neighbors tormented us. Jews desecrated Shabbat publicly, enslaved their fellow Jews and intermarried with the local population. Finally, after almost two hundred years, the Hasmoneans succeeded in restoring independence to *Am Yisrael* and purifying the *Beit HaMikdash*. In our generation, too, the third redemption is a slow process. Compared to our past history, the progress is rapid, but it is certainly not an instantaneous redemption. How long will this continue? It all depends on us. The more we dedicate ourselves to the task, the sooner we will achieve the Kingdom of Israel and the ideal Jewish State.

The Mitzva of Eretz Yisrael

The mitzva of Eretz Yisrael according to Ramban

Is having our own State in *Eretz Yisrael* a means to an end, or an end in itself? Does the State possess inherent value and holiness, or is it merely a way to accomplish certain goals, such as the observance of *mitzvot*? Is it no more than a place to achieve security for the Jews – a "safe haven," to quote Theodor Herzl? If so, then there may be times when we can achieve these goals better somewhere else. We may come to the conclusion that Jews are safer in the Diaspora than they are in *Eretz Yisrael*, or that it is easier to observe the Torah outside of *Eretz Yisrael*. If this is the case, are we to give up the idea of a Jewish State?

To answer this question, we must first clarify how *Halacha* relates to the State, because *Halacha* is the system that enables us to put the Torah's ideals into practice. *Ramban*, who categorized the *halachot* pertaining to *Eretz Yisrael* and the State of Israel, derived our halachic obligations regarding the Land from the verse, "And you shall inherit it [*Eretz Yisrael*] and you shall live in it."[8] This general *mitzva* includes three related stages:

1 It is a *mitzva* to live in *Eretz Yisrael* and not in the Diaspora. This *mitzva* is incumbent upon every individual Jew.
2 It is a *mitzva* to build up *Eretz Yisrael* and to make it flourish: "We may not allow it to remain desolate."[9] This *mitzva* is directed to the nation and not to individuals. Not every Jew is a contractor or a farmer (though doctors and teachers also play important roles in developing the country). Therefore, it is the nation as a whole that is responsible

for the population and development of all parts of the Land, by creating cities and villages, and developing agriculture and industry.

3 It is a *mitzva* to possess *Eretz Yisrael*: "And we are forbidden to allow it to be ruled by any other nation."[10] *Eretz Yisrael* must belong to, and be under the sovereignty of, *Am Yisrael*, and not be ruled by any other nation. This *mitzva*, too, is incumbent upon the nation, and not upon individuals.[11] Sovereignty of a nation over its land is the definition of a state. Therefore, the Torah commands us to establish a sovereign Jewish State in *Eretz Yisrael*.[12]

A mitzva for every generation, even in exile

We might think that this *mitzva* applied only to the days when we entered *Eretz Yisrael* with Yehoshua, or to the period when King David conquered the Land, and that it is not relevant to us today. After all, God sent Assyria and Babylonia to destroy the Kingdom of Israel, resulting in *Am Yisrael's* exile. Perhaps this is a sign that He no longer wishes us to have a sovereign State in *Eretz Yisrael*. *Ramban*, however, reiterates three times that the *mitzvot* of conquering *Eretz Yisrael* and settling it apply throughout all generations, even during our exile.

It is incorrect to presume that our current dispersion indicates that God doesn't want us to leave the Diaspora and establish a State. If it is a *mitzva*, no difficulty or obstacle can erase our obligation. We cannot use difficult events as an excuse not to fulfill a *mitzva*. This may be compared to a person who is about to write out a check for charity, when suddenly his pen runs out of ink. Is this a sign that he should not give make a donation? No, it is a sign that he should get a new pen! Despite the temporary setback, it is still a *mitzva* to give charity. If someone mistakenly transgresses the Shabbat laws, is that a sign that that person is incapable of observing Shabbat? No, it is a warning to be more careful and study the laws. When we experience difficulty in fulfilling any *mitzva*, we are simply being told to try harder, even if it may take a long time until we see the results of our efforts.

Some of the *mitzvot* which require the greatest exertion, and take the longest to bear fruit, are Torah study, prayer, acts of lovingkindness, and settling *Eretz Yisrael*.[13] Before Yehoshua entered *Eretz Yisrael*, God urged him to "be strong and courageous,"[14] signifying that it was going to be a major undertaking. We never received *Eretz Yisrael* on a silver platter in the past, and our task today is no less fraught with difficulty. We might wonder why *Ramban* himself did not try to establish a State in *Eretz Yisrael*. In his time, conditions were not conducive for its fulfillment. *Halacha* terms this phenomenon as one's "force of circumstance." One who is unable to perform a *mitzva* is not exempt from it; he is simply not liable to punishment. We must keep on persisting throughout the generations, until we succeed in fulfilling this *mitzva*.

Rambam: The mitzva to appoint a king

In his addenda to *Rambam's Sefer HaMitzvot*, *Ramban* inserts the *mitzva* of possessing *Eretz Yisrael* and establishing sovereignty over it. *Rambam* himself, however, did not include this *mitzva* there as one of the 613 *mitzvot*. Yet, in his *Mishneh Torah*, he does state that it is a *mitzva* to live in *Eretz Yisrael*, and that this *mitzva* is as important as all the others combined. In fact, it is so important that one spouse can legally force the other to fulfill it.[15] Therefore, its conspicuous omission from the *Sefer HaMitzvot* is significant and requires explanation.

We do find that *Rambam* considers the appointing of a king over *Am Yisrael* a *mitzva* and includes it in his *Sefer HaMitzvot*.[16] Obviously, there can be no king unless there is a nation over which to rule. If *Am Yisrael* does not live in its homeland – or is ruled by another nation – this *mitzva* is meaningless. Therefore, the *mitzva* of appointing a king includes within it the obligation to establish a sovereign State of Israel for *Am Yisrael* who resides there. The term "king" does not necessarily mean a king in the narrow sense of the word, but refers to any authoritative leadership agreed upon by the nation as a whole. This government has all the power and authority of a king. The laws concerning rebellion against a king are deduced from Yehoshua, who was the leader of *Am Yisrael*, but nevertheless was not officially its king.[17] For example, Yehoshua was told, "Any man who rebels against you...shall be killed."[18] Although he was not formally a king, defying his orders was deemed "rebellion against the king" because he was the national leader.[19]

The Israeli government of today falls into the same category. Since it is elected by the people, it is empowered to make national decisions. The sovereignty of the State of Israel is certainly not a true kingship; it is a government and not a monarchy. Moreover, it is not run according to religious principles. Despite this, our government has some of the authority of a king of Israel,[20] and is part of the necessary groundwork for fulfillment of the *mitzva* of establishing the Kingdom of Israel. This is a long and arduous process, consisting of many phases, which will ultimately culminate in the Kingdom of the House of David.

Independence signifies rejuvenation and its loss signifies destruction

Loss of an independent State in *Eretz Yisrael* is the halachic definition of destruction. According to *Halacha*, "One who sees the cities of Judah in their destruction must tear his clothes."[21] R. Yosef Karo writes, "As long as the cities are ruled by non-Jews – even if they are settled by Jews – they are termed 'destroyed.'"[22] In other words, despite the fact that the cities of *Eretz Yisrael* are populated by Jews, if non-Jews rule them, their halachic status is one of "destruction." If, on the other hand, Jews control the cities, they are considered "built," even if no one lives there. Therefore, we do not tear our clothes today over the sight of any cities, standing or destroyed, that are under Israeli jurisdiction.

In 1967, after the Six Day War, R. Zvi Yehuda Kook ruled that we should no longer tear our clothes upon the sight of the Temple Mount, since it is under Israeli jurisdiction. We have the political power to rebuild the *Beit HaMikdash* today. The fact that we have no immediate plans to do so, for various religious, political and other reasons (justified or not), does not negate the fact that it is *our* decision not to build the *Beit HaMikdash*, and therefore we no longer tear our clothes when we see the Temple Mount, as we would if it were under non-Jewish domination.[23]

Loss of independence and exile also constitute the destruction of the Torah. There are those who say, "The Torah alone is sufficient; there is no need for a State. We managed very well without our own State for two thousand years." Our Sages were not of this opinion. They explained, "Her [Zion's] king and princes are [scattered] among the nations – there is no Torah. There is no greater nullification of Torah than the exile of Israel." They did not intend us to take this statement to mean that we need devote less time to studying Torah in the Diaspora. They meant that the exile invalidates the essence and purpose of the Torah, which can only be realized when *Am Yisrael* is in its homeland.

Independence equals peace

Another halachic reference to national independence as an ideal may be found in the laws of fast days. The prophets declared four national fast days: the Seventeenth of *Tammuz*, the Ninth of *Av*, the Fast of Gedalia, and the Tenth of *Tevet*. The prophet Zecharia promised us that in the future, these fast days will become days of joy.[24] The Talmud expands upon this, listing three possible permutations regarding our obligation to fast on these days:

1 In times of peace – these will be days of joy.
2 In times of oppression – these remain fast days.
3 When there is neither peace nor oppression, fasting is optional; it is not an obligatory *mitzva*.[25]

However, the earliest halachic authorities wrote that regarding the Ninth of *Av* – when so many tragedies occurred – the nation voluntarily accepted upon itself the obligation to fast from sunset to sunset with accompanying restrictions. On the other three fast days, we also fast, but with certain leniencies – only from sunrise to sunset and without the added restrictions of the Ninth of *Av*. In any case, in times of real peace, we do not fast.

What is the definition of "peace"? According to *Ramban*, it refers to the time when the *Beit HaMikdash* is built. According to *Rashi*, it means "that the nations of the world do not rule Israel with a heavy hand."[26] In other words, we are autonomous and not subject to foreign rule. *Rashi's* definition of peace has no organic connection to the cessation of hostilities, but rather to autonomy. Even during times of war – as long as we have the ability to defend ourselves and fight back without losing our independence – according to *Rashi*, we are "at peace."

Rambam writes that the Jews even fasted on the Ninth of *Av* during the Second Temple Period, after the *Beit HaMikdash* had been rebuilt.[27] The *Admor* of Gur explains that *Rambam* follows *Rashi's* definition of peace, which is determined by our independence from other nations. For most of the Second Temple Period, we were under foreign domination – first under Persian rule and then Greek and Roman rule. This period was defined as one in which "there was neither peace nor war," and in such a case, according to *Rashi*, the Jews should fast on the Ninth of *Av*, despite the fact that the *Beit HaMikdash* was standing. Only later, under the Maccabees, did we achieve self-rule. Therefore, *Rambam* rules that the Jews' lack of liberty during the Second Temple Period obligated them to fast, except for the brief period of Hasmonean rule.[28]

Today, the dove is the universally accepted symbol of peace. Where did this symbol originate? In our sources, the dove first appears in the story of Noach. He sent the dove out of the ark to find out whether the floodwaters had sufficiently dried up, and she returned to him in the evening with "an olive leaf in her mouth."[29] Our Sages commented: "The dove requested of God: Let my food be as bitter as a raw olive, but only dependent upon You, rather than as sweet as honey, but at the mercy of men."[30] The dove thereby revealed a desire for freedom, even at the price of self-sacrifice and inconvenience. Thus, the dove is the symbol of independence and of the willingness to sacrifice in order to achieve this aim. This is *Rashi*'s definition of peace: that no other nation will rule over us, even if we have to fight to preserve our freedom. According to this view, peace is not a state of "ceasefire," but rather one of independence *despite* the wars.

According to *Rashi*'s outlook on peace, it would seem that we should not fast in this generation, since we do have the State of Israel in our possession. Aren't we independent in our country, free from the domination of other nations? Aren't we at the stage of "peace," wherein the fast days are transformed into days of rejoicing? There are those who say that our independence isn't complete since we are not altogether free from the influence of the nations, as we are subject to political pressure. This is not a valid claim because all nations of the world are subject to such pressure; this does not make them any less independent. Rather, the reason that we still fast in our generation is because most of *Am Yisrael* is still in exile under the rule of other nations; hence, *Rashi*'s definition of peace does not apply to the whole nation.

These Are The Pangs of Birth

The sanctity of the State derives from the sanctity of the mitzvot

We can conclude that it is a *mitzva* to establish the State of Israel and consequently, this State has sanctity. Sanctity is the state of being which results from the performance of a *mitzva*. Sanctity is not an exalted, intangible concept; rather, it is precisely defined by the formulation, "who sanctified us through His *mitzvot*."[31] This certainly does not imply that everything that takes place in the State of Israel is holy, but rather that the establishment and continued existence of the State is a *mitzva*, the fulfillment of which constitutes its sanctity.

Therefore, on the fifth of *Iyar*, 5708, *Am Yisrael* as a whole fulfilled a wondrous *mitzva* by establishing a Jewish State in *Eretz Yisrael*. Although we do not declare a holiday on every day in which we fulfill *mitzvot*, the day on which a *mitzva* is performed for the first time is considered a joyous occasion. In a similar vein, a young person celebrates his or her *bar/bat mitzva* because it is the first opportunity to fulfill *mitzvot* in an obligatory, rather than a voluntary, manner.[32] Thus, Yom HaAtzmaut is celebrated as a holiday, as it is the day we first fulfilled the *mitzva* of renewing our sovereignty over *Eretz Yisrael*.

The sanctity of Yom HaAtzmaut

Why is Yom HaAtzmaut celebrated as a holiday? Because this is the day the State was declared. Consequently, the Arabs declared war at once and tried to wipe us off the face of the earth. The war was fought under extremely difficult conditions: enormous enemy forces, armed and experienced, attacked our small fledgling army, which was unskilled and without much ammunition *Am Yisrael* was in great danger, but with the help of God, and with unflagging dedication, we triumphed. It was a great miracle – we were saved, and the State survived and flourished.

It is a *mitzva* to thank God for His miracles and to commemorate them Therefore, we declared this day a holiday, both to commemorate the *mitzva* of establishing the State on that day, and to thank God for the miracle of *Am Yisrael's* salvation from the mortal danger that we faced during the War of Independence. This day of thanksgiving is sacred, since by observing it we fulfill the *mitzva* of thanking God for His miracles.

This was the basis for sanctifying Chanuka, Purim, and the other days mentioned in *Megillat Ta'anit*. Throughout the generations, Jewish communities have enacted many days of thanksgiving and celebration. If even local communities were empowered to establish such festivals, how much more appropriate is it to celebrate Yom HaAtzmaut, when a great miracle happened to the whole nation. The ordaining of a holiday on which to commemorate this miracle is a Torah obligation. Exactly how to mark the day – whether it be in the form of a festive meal, reciting *Hallel*, or other customs – is the responsibility of the Torah leaders of each generation to determine.

We may ask why no such "Independence Days" were established in the days of Yehoshua when *Am Yisrael* first came to *Eretz Yisrael*, or in the days of Ezra and Nechemia during the Return to Zion before the Second Temple was built? In point of fact, Pesach is the Independence Day marking our first entry into *Eretz Yisrael* during the time of Yehoshua. *Am Yisrael* was aware at the time that the Exodus from Egypt took place in order to bring us to *Eretz Yisrael*. God had promised us, "And I shall take you out from under the burdens of Egypt...and I shall save you...and I shall redeem you...and I shall take you...and I shall bring you to the land."[33] This is the ultimate goal: *Eretz Yisrael*. In Egypt, even before they left, they performed the Pesach sacrifice with their hips belted and their staffs at hand.[34] The women took drums with them because they were certain God would perform miracles and they would have the opportunity to sing His praises.[35] After the Egyptians drowned, *Am Yisrael* sang to God, "With Your mercy, You have led this nation whom You have redeemed; You have led them with Your strength to Your sanctified site."[36] They knew with certainty that the Lord, their Redeemer, was leading them to *Eretz Yisrael* to build the *Beit HaMikdash* there. The holiday of Pesach celebrates the Exodus from Egypt, the miracles at the sea and in the desert, and also the entry into *Eretz Yisrael*, for the sake of which all these miracles were performed.

During the period of Ezra and Nechemia, *Am Yisrael* did not declare a holiday, for they were not yet independent, but rather were subservient to Persia. Neither had they been saved from death. But about 200 years later, in the time of the Hasmoneans, *Am Yisrael* achieved independence and won a tremendous victory over the Greeks.[37] They then designated the days of Chanuka as a holiday in commemoration of the miracles which happened to them. Chanuka may thus be considered the "Independence Day" of the Second Temple Period.

The Spiritual Significance of the State

What is the aim of the *mitzva* to establish a sovereign State of Israel? Isn't the goal of the *Am Yisrael* to be a "light unto the nations"? Why should we need our own political entity in order to accomplish this, and why should we be defined within a limited body of territory? Isn't it preferable that we be dispersed throughout the world? Wouldn't we have more influence that way?

Mankind as a whole is obligated to develop the frameworks of society, economy, science, technology and culture. These are all important objectives, but they constitute only the external structure of our world. The main goal is to form the inner substance of life – and that is the responsibility of *Am Yisrael*. It would seem, then, that a sovereign State for the Jews is irrelevant in accomplishing this task.

Am Yisrael, however, can only fulfill its mandate of healing the spiritual illnesses of mankind as a nation. Just as there is always a nucleus of spiritual elite within each nation, so, too, is *Am Yisrael* the "kingdom of priests and a holy nation"[38] within the family of nations of the world. It is we who, as a people, must become "a light unto the nations." This was the situation in the days of King Shlomo – whose foreign and domestic policies enlightened the whole world – as illustrated by the visit of the Queen of Sheba, who was so impressed by his administration that "she had no spirit left."[39] This was a sanctification of the Divine name. The higher the level of the society we create in our Land, the greater the impact we will have on the rest of the world.

In order to achieve this, we must first become a normal, healthy nation. We must be united and independent in our own Land.[40] Based upon this foundation, we will then truly become "a holy nation," and thereby sanctify God's name throughout the world.

Sanctification of the Divine name is the highest value; desecration of His name is the most serious transgression. The world was created for the very purpose of sanctifying God's name. Sanctification of the Divine name in the spiritual world is the domain of the angels, while we do the same in the physical world. As we proclaim in the prayer of *Kedusha*, "Let us sanctify Your name in this world, as they do in the world above."

The exile of *Am Yisrael* from its own Land, and its dispersion in the Diaspora, is the greatest possible desecration of God's name. It is written in *Yechezkel*:

> Son of Man, the House of Israel were residing in their own land, and they defiled it…and I scattered them among the nations…and they desecrated My holy name when it was said about them, "This is the nation of God, and they have left His land."[41]

This desecration of God's name must be rectified:

> And I shall sanctify My great name, which has been desecrated before the nations, which you have desecrated in their midst…and I shall take you out of the nations and gather you from all the lands and I shall bring you to your land.[42]

The process of the ingathering to Zion is a great sanctification of God's name – rectifying the earlier desecration of His name caused by the exile – through the fulfillment of the Divine plan to establish "a kingdom of priests and a holy nation" in *Eretz Yisrael*.

The partial participation of Am Yisrael

Why didn't all Jews, particularly the religious ones, immigrate to *Eretz Yisrael* immediately after the State was established?

This is, indeed, a good question. We have noted that redemption has always been a gradual process. Even in the time of Moshe Rabbeinu, only one-fifth of the population left Egypt. Most Jews – 80 percent! – had no desire to leave, and died during the Plague of Darkness.[43] Later, most of that generation, except for Yehoshua and Calev, were afraid to enter *Eretz Yisrael*. They cried and wanted to return to Egypt, and in the end, they all died in the desert, despite all the miracles performed on their behalf, and despite the leadership of Moshe Rabbeinu.

In the same way, only a small number of Jews came to *Eretz Yisrael* in the time of Ezra and Nechemia, even though they knew that the allotted seventy years of exile were up. The prophets Chagai, Zecharia and Malachi called upon them in the name of God to immigrate, but they were in no hurry. This is the meaning of the verse, "I am asleep, but my heart is awake. I hear my beloved knock. Open the door, my sister...."[44] In exile, *Am Yisrael* slept, but the prophets (the "heart") were awake and tried to stir the nation. The Holy One – the Beloved – knocked on the door, using the prophets as His mouthpiece, but no one answered.[45] Later, Zerubavel returned to *Eretz Yisrael* with a few thousand Jews, then Ezra with another few thousand, and finally Nehemia with a few thousand more. Altogether, about 42,000 Jews immigrated to *Eretz Yisrael*.[46] Where was everyone else? They all stayed behind in Babylonia. Today as well, there is no sudden rush of Jewish *aliya*. Bit by bit, Jews trickle to *Eretz Yisrael* – one from this family, two from that city.

This is human nature. People find it hard to rise above a way of thinking they've grown up with. It takes time to absorb new ideas and to integrate them. It is also hard for people to leave the security and familiarity of their homes, work and *yeshivot*. Because of these difficulties, people invent excuses to answer the question of why they don't immigrate to *Eretz Yisrael*. The plain and simple truth is that it is very hard to do. We understand the difficulty, but we cannot condone it. The challenges of *aliya* are an explanation as to why so few Jews immigrate, but they are not a justification. We must do everything we can to enable Jews to make *aliya*.

Sometimes, we, ourselves, are to blame for people not making *aliya*, because we do not adequately absorb the immigrants. We do not make enough of an effort to help them find employment and housing. We poke fun at them. Each new wave of immigrants, after they become settled, mock the new immigrants as they themselves were mocked: first the Moroccans, then the Georgians, the Ethiopians, and the Russians. We must do more to successfully absorb new immigrants.

The State of Israel was not established as a mitzva

Once, in Bnei Brak, I decided to learn for a few hours in R. Ashlag's *yeshiva*. He was an expert in Kabbala, a Zionist and a holy rabbi, and celebrated Yom HaAtzmaut with a festive meal every year. At the end of volume 21 of the *Sulam* commentary on the Zohar, written by his father, the first R. Ashlag, there is an article about Yom HaAtzmaut. I began to search for that volume, and the *yeshiva* students gathered around me to see what I was looking for. "Volume 21," I answered. "What? On Yom HaAtzmaut? Why look for that article?" they said mockingly. "Your rabbi, not I, wrote that article," I answered. "No," they retorted, "it is in our rabbi's merit that we study Torah, but that does not mean we have to accept all his ideas. In this case we choose to follow a different path from his. Anyway, what reason is there to celebrate Yom HaAtzmaut?" I answered, "It is the fulfillment of the *mitzva* to establish a State and to settle Jews here, which is incumbent upon *Am Yisrael*."

"But those who established the State had no intention of fulfilling any *mitzva*," one objected. "Not every *mitzva* has to be performed intentionally,"[47] I answered. Another protested, "But if their intention was expressly *not* to perform a *mitzva*, then surely that act is not considered a *mitzva*?[48] In fact, this State was established for the very purpose of destroying the Torah." I denied that allegation, but another *yeshiva* student added, "It is the '*sitra achra*" (the devil) who established the State." "The devil is also one of God's creations," I countered. The students were taken aback, but one of the older ones said, "He's right!" and they began arguing with one another. I took advantage of the tumult to make my exit, as it was clear that I would not find a quiet place to study there.

It is true that the founders of the State were not motivated by the idea of fulfilling a *mitzva*. It is true that it is far preferable to fulfill *mitzvot* out of a desire to perform God's will, but a *mitzva* which is done without this intent is still considered a *mitzva*.[49]

Continuing problems in the mitzva of establishing the State

There are many things amiss within the State of Israel that require attention, in the fields of justice, education, and so forth. Do not these flaws thus negate the value of a Jewish State? Isn't the State supposed to be the foundation of "a kingdom of priests and a holy nation?" Doesn't the spiritual regression we see in *Eretz Yisrael* delegitimize the existence of such a State? This common misconception has to be corrected. The sanctity of the State does not derive from that fact that it is the means to a spiritual goal. No justification is necessary for the existence of the State; rather, its sanctity derives from its very existence, which is the fulfillment of the *mitzva* of establishing a sovereign Jewish State in *Eretz Yisrael*. Performance of any *mitzva* has sanctity, no matter what happens in its aftermath. For example, we fulfill the *mitzva* to "be fruitful and multiply" when we marry and have children. Even if our children grow up to be bad people (God forbid), this does not in any way invalidate the *mitzva* we have fulfilled. Perhaps we have failed in the *mitzva* of educating them, but we have still fulfilled the *mitzva* of giving life. It is our obligation to fulfill every *mitzva* we can, without indulging in convoluted calculations regarding the possible outcomes of our actions. The very act of fulfilling a *mitzva* contains its own sanctity because our Creator "has sanctified us with His *mitzvot*."

Consider the following parable: A person erects a *sukka*, only to talk falsehood and *lashon hara* in it all day long. These actions are serious transgressions, but they in no way invalidate his *sukka*. This person has fulfilled the *mitzva* of sitting in the *sukka*, while incidentally sinning in his speech. The *mitzva* of *Eretz Yisrael* can be compared in many ways to the *mitzva* of *sukka*: "And His *sukka* was in Shalem, and His dwelling place in Zion."[50] The sanctity of the State is expressed through the sovereign control of *Eretz Yisrael* by *Am Yisrael*, with the help of the Israeli army. The existence of the State, in and of itself, is a *mitzva*, and transgressions performed within it do not invalidate its sanctity.

It is obvious that fulfilling the *mitzva* of sitting in the *sukka* does not in any way sanction any transgressions committed there. In the same way, one is not permitted to transgress a commandment by virtue of the fact that one lives in *Eretz Yisrael*. Conversely, sins committed in *Eretz Yisrael* cannot invalidate the sanctity of the State, just as talking *lashon hara* in a *sukka* cannot nullify the *mitzva* of sitting in the *sukka*. It is a despicable act, but the person has still, nonetheless, fulfilled the *mitzva* of sitting in the *sukka*.

The spiritual upheaval is not connected to the establishment of the State

In truth, the spiritual problems we see today in *Eretz Yisrael* have nothing to do with the establishment of the State. About 200 years ago, for various reasons which we cannot go into here, there was a universal religious and moral upheaval that affected Judaism as well. The founders of the State, and the waves of immigration that followed, brought their spiritual crises and difficulties with them. The State did not cause them, nor is it responsible for their continued existence within its framework. The same spiritual regression, to a much greater extent, exists in the Diaspora. There, the result is assimilation, whereas here, in the Jewish State, it is possible to overcome the crises and resolve the problems. Saying, "It would be better not to have the State if this is what it looks like," is like saying to someone eating nonkosher food in a *sukka*, "You would be better off not sitting in the *sukka* if you're going to eat nonkosher food." Outside the *sukka*, he would certainly be eating nonkosher food! It has no connection to the *sukka*. On the contrary, perhaps in time, the sanctity of the *sukka* will influence him to stop eating nonkosher food.

The prophet Yechezkel said in God's name, "I shall bring you to your land...and I shall sprinkle you with pure waters...and I shall remove your heart of stone and I shall give you a heart of flesh."[51] Who are those who immigrated to *Eretz Yisrael* and built our State? Impure people with hearts of stone, but here, in *Eretz Yisrael*, they shall be perfected. This will not happen instantaneously. The crisis which began 200 years ago caused deep wounds. We have not yet succeeded in creating the tools to educate this new personality type towards faith in God. Moreover, many of us don't even understand what happened and what the roots of this spiritual crisis are. It may take many years to repair the damage, maybe even as long as the crisis has lasted – 200 years. In any case, not only is the establishment of the State not the cause of this crisis, but it may even be part of the solution.

These are the pangs of birth

Zionism is at its very beginning. We find ourselves at the start of the Redemption, or perhaps the middle of it, certainly not at its end or after it. We have always known that the Redemption would come gradually, one stage at a time. The *Talmud Yerushalmi* recounts that several Sages were once watching a sunrise. Said one, "Such is Israel's Redemption, bit by bit."[52] The light doesn't flood the world all at once. Rather, light and dark are at first mixed, struggling with each other, until finally light is victorious.

Each side seeks the good of the nation, each thinks it is saving the country and the other is destroying it. Precisely when the conflict is so great, we must remember that we are one people. *Maharal* of Prague, at the beginning of his book *Netzach Yisrael*, contrasts the natural, healthy situation of a people – that is, a situation of Redemption – with the unhealthy, unnatural state of exile. In exile, we are scattered, lacking independence and a homeland. In Redemption, we are together, independent, and in our own Land. Bringing the nation together, in other words, is the essence of Redemption. For that reason, when the Declaration of Independence was signed by representatives of the left and the right, the Orthodox and the secular, it was a vital stage in the rebirth of the nation.

Today as well, everyone has the right and obligation to stand up for his or her views, but without crossing crucial lines – without violence, hatred or disrespect. This isn't the first time our people has been torn between opposing opinions – religious Zionists versus post-Zionists, Hagana versus Irgun, supporters and opponents of accepting German reparations. There is room for debate between opposing beliefs – as long as we remember that we are brothers. We must do our utmost to increase the sense of brotherhood in our Land.

Our nation has aspired to great heights, and, through its determination, has achieved great successes. Beneath the external difficulties and despair, we believe there is a tremendous holiness which will overcome all flaws. Beneath the religious cynicism lies hidden faith; beneath the hatred lies brotherhood; beneath the darkness is a great light, which will eventually drive away all the shadows.

R. Avraham Yitzchak Kook once said to a visitor from America, "You have to make *aliya*. Can't you see how terribly dark the situation is for Judaism in your country?" The visitor replied, "And in *Eretz Yisrael* there are no crises?!" The Rabbi said, "Certainly there are, but you see your crises as death throes; we see ours as birth pangs."

Lag B'Omer

The Sin of Disrespect

THE TALMUD RELATES that R. Akiva's students died between the holidays of Pesach and Shavuot because they did not treat each other with respect.[1] The day the dying ceased was Lag B'Omer, the 33rd day of *Sefirat HaOmer*.[2]

How are we to understand this? How could Torah scholars deteriorate to such a low level of mutual disrespect that they deserved to die? We would surely expect that in the *yeshiva* of R. Akiva, whose primary teaching was, "Love your neighbor as yourself[3] – that is the main principle of the whole Torah",[4] his students would be the embodiment of brotherly love. To explain this mystery, we would have to assume that these students grew up with serious social deficiencies, and purposely chose to study in R. Akiva's *yeshiva* in order to learn brotherly love and respect. However, the *yeshiva* did not completely succeed in this task, and some remnants of disrespect lingered – for which 24,000 students were punished by death.

Violence is inherent in idol worship

R. Menachem Azaria of Pano, the rabbi of the western school of Kabbala and a student of R. Moshe Cordovero, writes that there is a connection between the death of the 24,000 students of R. Akiva and the 24,000 Israelites who died in the plague after worshiping Ba'al Peor.[5] It is written:

> And Israel dwelled in Shittim, and the people began to stray with the daughters of Moab. And the Moabite women called on them to sacrifice to their gods, and the people ate and bowed down to their gods. And Israel

became very much attached to Ba'al Peor, and God was angry at Israel....
And those who died in the plague numbered 24,000.[6]

Idolatry is a violent phenomenon, and idolaters themselves are, by definition, violent people. Idolatry is not merely an ideological error; it also carries with it an immoral outlook. As with any belief system that has a philosophical foundation, there are practical and moral implications. As G.K. Chesterton wrote in the introduction to his book, *The Heretics*, "Belief is the most practical thing there is." Idolatry is a philosophy of life that legitimizes all of mankind's basest urges. Idolaters do not view these urges as flaws to be corrected; on the contrary, inflamed passions are, to them, a sign of vigorous health and a life lived according to nature.

Nietzsche represents one such school of philosophy – admiration of might and unrepressed, natural passion. He compares two gods of Greek mythology: Apollo, who sits at the helm of his chariot in a dignified manner, guiding the sun; and Bacchus, who spends all his time drinking wine and having orgies with his disciples. One might think that the first figure is more worthy of admiration, but Nietzsche believes differently. He considers Apollo to be weak and pale, whereas Bacchus, who is controlled by his desires and adulterous by nature, is praiseworthy. He is the "natural man" who "lets it all hang out." The philosophy is: Mankind, if you are sexually aroused, don't hold back. On the contrary, your lust is sacred. There are prostitutes in the temples of the gods and sexual relations are part of their service. Do you lust to spill blood? Good, that is also a way of serving the gods. Sacrifice your son to Molech. Do you want to relieve yourself? You need not be ashamed; no one is an angel. There is no need to be modest. Show off your excrement – that is also a way of serving the gods, as in "Ba'al Peor" (Hebrew for "Master of Excrement"). Follow your desires, be true to yourself: honest, intimate, natural. Let life flow with no inhibitions. This belief system idealizes all the base passions natural to mankind. Therefore, our Sages warned us that pagans are dangerous and prone to violence, and one should be on one's guard against them.[7]

In recent generations, the violent behavior of paganism has reawakened. Anything goes; the important thing is to obey all natural instincts. This is the romantic, neo-pagan approach of Nietzsche, and to a certain extent also of Freud, but it has become universal. To varying degrees, this philosophy has influenced us all.

Sexual permissiveness is another form of violent behavior. A woman becomes a sex object instead of a human being. There are women who dress well in order to sexually attract the men around them. Why do they do this? Is a woman a window display? Is she an object designed to provide pleasure to others? This approach debases a woman's intrinsic value as a person.

The main point of idolatry is thus an outburst of violent instincts of various types. Every human being has egotistic tendencies: "I am, and there is no one else of significance." "You're in my way. I'll push you aside and eliminate you." These tendencies must be corrected.

Shimon and Levi at Ba'al Peor

Two characters with an inherited capacity for violence meet at Ba'al Peor: Zimri ben Salu, prince of the tribe of Shimon, and Pinchas ben Elazar HaKohen of the tribe of Levi. Their forefathers had killed a whole city: "And the two sons of Yaakov, Shimon and Levi, the brothers of Dina, took up their swords and attacked the city, sure of their own safety, and killed every male."[8] Shechem had raped their sister and so, in their rage, they killed every male in the city. *Rambam* explains that Shimon and Levi's actions had halachic justification, for the residents of the city should have taken Shechem to task for his reprehensible behavior. Since the people did not judge him, and doing justice is one of the seven *mitzvot* given to Bnei Noach, they deserved to be put to death for this severe failure.[9]

Yaakov, however, was displeased with the actions of two sons and this is reflected in his blessing to them on his deathbed:

> Shimon and Levi are brothers; instruments of cruelty are their swords. Let my soul not join their council; to their gatherings let my honor not be united, for in their anger, they slew a man, and according to their desire they lamed an ox. Cursed be their anger, for it is fierce, and their wrath, for it is cruel. I will divide them in Yaakov and scatter them in Israel.[10]

His condemnation refers not to the act of murder itself, which may have been morally and legally justified, but rather to the fact that they did it out of impulsive rage. This he aimed to correct by scattering them among the other tribes in order to dilute their violent tendencies.

As the generations passed, the tribe of Levi did rise above this tendency to impulsive violence. When *Bnei Yisrael* sinned with the Golden Calf, Moshe called, "Who is for God – come to me," and the tribe of Levi volunteered. They killed those who had bowed down to the Golden Calf, even their relatives. This heroic action caused them to be chosen as those who would serve in the *Beit HaMikdash*,[11] and to be blessed by Moshe Rabbeinu on his deathbed.[12]

Why were these killings considered praiseworthy? Although their actions involved force and violence, they were carried out in order to achieve justice. A sovereign state and its arms of government, police and army, are permitted to use force to execute justice. This is essential, for otherwise it would be impossible to run a country. Of course, only the minimum force necessary may be used. Criminals must be brought to justice, and jailed or fined, but they must not be humiliated unnecessarily. *Rambam*, after specifying the courts' authority to punish, qualifies their powers: "In all ways must they act for the sake of Heaven; they must not show disrespect for creatures of God."[13] Similarly, the tribe of Levi carried out the orders of Moshe and of God following the sin of the Golden Calf. Their capabilities for force had been refined and channeled properly.

Unfortunately, the tribe of Shimon did not succeed in modulating their tendency to violence. At Ba'al Peor, the two tribes met. The violent prince of the tribe of Shimon, Zimri ben Salu, was confronted by Pinchas HaKohen of the tribe of Levi, a noble, merciful and peaceful person. During this particular crisis, Pinchas realized that drastic action was needed in order to avert greater national disaster. The two clashed; Pinchas overcame Zimri, and Divine wrath at *Bnei Yisrael* was abated, but only after 24,000 died in a plague.

Our spiritual inheritance throughout the generations

The deaths of those who committed idolatry at Ba'al Peor did not eradicate the problem. Jailing thieves, killing murderers, and punishing criminals are not real solutions. The fact that crime exists indicates that society as a whole has spiritual and moral flaws. These faults manifest themselves more strongly in certain members of society, who become criminals. When Tel Aviv was first founded, no one locked his or her door at night. As the State developed, undesirable elements became more common, just as dregs always sink to the bottom in the process of wine maturation.[14] Today, we have no shortage of criminals. Those who are brought to justice are simply the most blatant examples of corruption in our midst; they represent the general weaknesses and violent tendencies within our society. We are not a violent or corrupt nation as a whole, but the problem does exist. We must correct our faults; if we do not, they will be bequeathed to future generations.

All our successes and failures throughout history are passed down from one generation to the next: "God visits the sins of the fathers upon the sons…and does mercy to thousands [of generations]."[15] This is because all the generations are part of one entity. Viewing history as a disconnected process leads to the mistaken attitude that "I live now; he lived at a different time. We belong to this generation; they belonged to another." However, if we see everything as interconnected, then all of *Am Yisrael*, throughout all generations, is part of one soul. Similarly, all humanity is part of one soul – the soul of Adam. And this single soul reveals itself in infinite variations throughout the generations, but they all strive to perfect themselves. Whatever is not clarified and corrected in one generation is passed onto the next. Whatever you have not accomplished will be left for someone else to do.

There are those who say, "What do I care? Let someone else do it!" But who is that "someone else"? It is you! We are all part of one unit. One who says, "Let someone else do it," may be compared to someone whose left hand drops something and says, "What do I care? Let the right hand pick it up!" The *Talmud Yerushalmi* comments on the commandment not to take vengeance with the following parable: One who takes revenge on a friend who has harmed him is like one whose one hand injures the other, and that hand then injures the first.[16] This holds true for *Am Yisrael* in each and every generation. Our Sages said, "Yitzchak can be called Avraham, Yitzchak can be called Yaakov, Avraham can be called Yaakov, it's all part of the same thing."[17] The unique Divine character of *Am Yisrael* appears differently in each generation. Each generation inherits all the good and all the bad of those that preceded it, and can be said to be the sum total of all preceding generations.

Why does God "visit the sins of the fathers upon the sons"? Why should we suffer for our fathers' sins? In truth, the positive heritage we receive is much greater than the negative one, as it says, "[God] does mercy to *thousands* of generations."[18] All the Torah and holiness, all the culture and progress of previous generations, is accessible to us. Can we refuse to inherit the "sting" along with the "honey" – the bad along with the good? To do so would mean to revert to hanging from trees and cutting food with sharp stones. We have inherited tremendous spiritual-ethical-cultural assets from past generations, and we have likewise inherited faults which we must correct. We should not consider it as "them" and "us." We are all part of the collective soul of *Am Yisrael* which is growing stronger from one generation to the next. Whatever is not rectified in this generation will continue to be a burden on the whole nation until such time as it is corrected in the future.[19]

There is a parable ascribed to R. Meir which illustrates the idea of mutual spiritual responsibility over the generations:

> Once there was a fox who was attacked by a lion. The fox suggested, "If you eat me, your hunger will not be satiated. Come with me and I'll show you a fat man who will satisfy your hunger." There was a covered pit, and a man was sitting behind it and praying. When the lion saw him, he said to the fox, "I'm afraid that his prayers will be my undoing." The fox answered, "Neither you nor your son need fear, only your grandson. Satiate your hunger now, and let your grandson worry in due time." The lion fell for the trick, leaped, and fell into the pit. The fox came over to the edge of the pit and looked down. The lion said, "Didn't you promise that the punishment would not smite until the third generation?" The fox answered, "But your grandfather also sinned, and you are being punished for his sin." The lion asked, "Is that fair?" The fox retorted, "Why didn't you think of that before?"[20]

Likewise, the phenomenon of idol worship first appeared at Ba'al Peor, but the death of the 24,000 idol worshipers at that time did not eradicate this failing on the part of *Am Yisrael*. The wild aggressiveness of idolatry continued to oppress their spirit from one generation to the next, all the way down to the generation of R. Akiva.

The bald-headed R. Akiva – erasing aggressiveness

In his youth, R. Akiva himself was somewhat belligerent. As an ignorant man (*am ha'aretz*) he was known to say, "I would love to take a bite out of a *talmid chacham*"[21] – or in today's slang, "I would love to break his bones!" This is verbal violence, as is the nature of Ben Azzai's praises of R. Akiva, "All the Sages of Israel are worth no more than a garlic peel except for that bald guy."[22] Why does Ben Azzai refer to R. Akiva in such a derogatory way while praising his wisdom? It must be that Ben Azzai did not intend to be insulting, but rather that he was referring to R. Akiva's approach: R. Akiva totally wiped out – "made bald" – his opposition.

The prophet Elisha was also called a bald man. As he was going to Beit El, youths came out and called after him, "Go, you bald man. Go, you bald man!" Elisha cursed them, and two bears came out of the forest and attacked forty-two of the children."[23] He created "a bald spot" among the children that day. Korach did the same when he caused the death of the many people who joined his revolt.[24]

The prototype of the hostile "baldy" is Cain. He only had one brother, but that brother argued with him and therefore was eliminated. That was Cain's approach: I will get rid of anyone I don't identify with or who bothers me. For that reason, even before he murdered his brother, Cain's offering was not accepted by God – because he was violent. His violence didn't first manifest itself at the murder of his brother; it was the pre-existing cause.[25] In contrast, Elisha means "*Eli sha* – My God has heard [me]." Even though Elisha and Cain look similar on the surface, Elisha was accepted by God, whereas Cain was not. In any case, Elisha, R. Akiva and Ben Azzai are all considered "bald" types – assertive enough to create a bald spot on the opposition.

R. Akiva was descended from converts.[26] There is one opinion that claims he was a descendant of the wicked Haman, as it is written, "The descendants of Haman studied Torah in Bnei Brak."[27] Who was in Bnei Brak at the time? R. Akiva, as it is written, "Follow the Sages to their *yeshiva*…follow R. Akiva to Bnei Brak."[28] Thus, R. Akiva was descended from Haman, who was descended from Amalek, who was descended from Eisav.

Eisav was the most brutal character in history. The day that Avraham died, and Eisav sold his birthright to Yaakov, Eisav is described as coming from the fields "tired."[29] Why was he so tired? Our Sages teach that on that day he had killed a man and raped a girl who was just about to be married, and committed other heinous transgressions.[30] Murder had exhausted him, as it is written in *Yirmiyahu*, "My soul is tired before the slayers."[31] His essence is captured in the blessing Yitzchak gave him, "You shall live by your sword"[32] – it is as if he is made of a sword. Amalek, Eisav's grandson, also epitomizes the violent person. His descendant, Haman, swears "to destroy, kill, and wipe out all the Jews, from youth to elderly, infant and woman, in one day."[33]

Nevertheless, we know that everything has its purpose, and in all things there is a spark of holiness. Regarding Amalek, the Torah commands us, "Wipe out the memory of Amalek from *beneath* the heavens,"[34] but not from above, in heaven itself. Even Amalek has a "heavenly source" which we are not to wipe out, but rather to love.[35] R. Shlomo of Lutzk, a disciple of the Maggid of Mezeritch, explains in his book, *Divrat Shlomo*, that the spark of divinity in Amalek is his intransigence: he doesn't allow for weakness or compromise.

This divine spark of Amalek was put to good use by R. Akiva, descendant of converts, descendant of Haman, descendant of Amalek, descendant of Eisav. He himself, before he studied Torah, wanted to break the bones of a *talmid chacham*, but he transformed himself, became a *ba'al teshuva* and taught the world to "Love your neighbor as yourself – that is the main principle of the whole Torah." Love is the solution to cruelty and aggression. For that reason, it is precisely the personality of R. Akiva which is best suited to correct that violent characteristic of *Am Yisrael* – through teaching his students to love. The problem of violence, which had been the heritage of *Am Yisrael* since the days of Ba'al Peor, was finally corrected in R. Akiva's generation. Twenty-four thousand students with aggressive tendencies came to study at his *yeshiva*. Under his tutelage, they refined their characters, purged themselves of wicked traits, and almost completely eliminated violent behavior. All that is left is that "they did not treat each other with respect." Compared to the situation at Ba'al Peor, with idolatry and sexual immorality rampant, the situation was greatly improved.

The remnants of violence that caused the destruction of the Beit HaMikdash
Mutual disrespect, however, is serious enough to delay the "light of the *Mashiach*."[36] The "light of the *Mashiach*" refers to a national order which emerges when there is a high level of mutual understanding and perception.

From this vantage point, we are able to see the good and honorable side of every creature and every being. But with a narrow perspective, we see only that which is unworthy and despicable. Thus, we mock and scorn our fellow Jews, delaying the appearance of the great light of the *Mashiach*.

As a nation, we have overcome the crude brutality of idolatry, adultery and murder. However, remnants of violence still remain and they take the form of mutual lack of respect. For this more subtle form of violence, the students of R. Akiva were punished very harshly. Disrespect is connected to baseless hatred, which was so widespread during the Second Temple Period that it caused the destruction of the *Beit HaMikdash*. *Netziv* explains that baseless hatred means abhorrence of anyone who has a different outlook:[37] "I am a Zionist, but you aren't." "You wear a black *kippa*, and I wear a knitted *kippa*." The "other" is construed to be an enemy of *Am Yisrael*, someone who has to be eliminated. Most people are not innately murderous, but some are easily misled into thinking that they are fighting a holy war against evildoers, whereas, in reality, they are entrapped in baseless hatred.

The Torah does not permit one who has been beaten or insulted to hate the attacker, though it does permit hitting back in self-defense. If this person does succumb to hate, it is still not considered baseless hatred. But one who hates another simply due to a different world view has become enmeshed in baseless hatred. Likewise, when people do not treat each other with respect, it's a sign that they are focusing on their differences, and not on what they have in common. This awakens feelings of revulsion and loathing between them. The contempt and causeless hatred which were not eradicated in the generation of R. Akiva led to the destruction of the Second *Beit HaMikdash* in the same generation. The problem of baseless hatred still exists in some measure today. It may take tens or even hundreds of generations until the last vestiges of violence disappear.

The significance of the customs of mourning during Sefirat HaOmer
We adopt certain mourning rituals during the *Sefirat HaOmer* period, such as not performing weddings, not cutting hair, and not buying new clothing or eating fruit that one has not yet partaken of that season (so as not to recite the *Shehecheyanu* blessing).[38] These customs are not identical to the regular rituals of mourning. For example, one who is mourning the death of a fam-

ily member is allowed to recite *Shehecheyanu* during the *Shiva* period. The customs of mourning during *Sefirat HaOmer* are also by no means absolute prohibitions. For example, though it has become customary to refrain from holding weddings during this period, according to the letter of *Halacha*, they are permitted.[39]

The *Sefirat HaOmer* period is a time of judgment, as it is written in the Mishna: "The wicked in hell are judged from Pesach to Shavuot."[40] During this period, the yields of fruit and grain in *Eretz Yisrael* are also determined.[41] Since this is a time of judgment, we would do well to act cautiously and refrain from all sin. The students of R. Akiva did not treat each other well all year round, but it was specifically during this period that they were punished.[42]

The period between Pesach and Shavuot is also the time of *Am Yisrael's* preparation for *Matan Torah*. They are like the seven clean days that a woman waits before she goes to the *mikva*. Therefore, we must be careful not to spoil these days of heightened awareness with frivolous, lighthearted behavior which may cause us to act unwisely. Careless laughter and festivity can lead to more serious transgressions. Thus, the mourning customs we observe during *Sefirat HaOmer* may be viewed as precautionary measures during this solemn period of judgment.

Yom Yerushalayim

Jerusalem is Not Mentioned in the Torah

WHAT DOES JERUSALEM mean to us? For some people the word conjures up memories; for others, it represents the history of *Am Yisrael*; for still others, it means the capital of *Eretz Yisrael*. Is there, however, a deeper significance to Jerusalem than the aforementioned aspects?

Turning to the Torah for an answer, we are confronted with a mystery, for nowhere in the Torah does the word "*Yerushalayim*" appear. How can the center of Jewish life and thought not be mentioned even once in the Torah?! It does, however, appear indirectly: "To the place which the Lord your God will choose – from within all your tribes – to set His name there; there shall you seek His dwelling place and come there."[1] The "place" had been chosen, but was still unnamed. In *Shirat HaYam* – the song of *Am Yisrael* at the Splitting of the Sea – Moshe sang, "You shall bring them in and plant them on the mountain of Your legacy, the place which You have made to dwell in."[2] There is a mountain which is God's legacy, but the Torah does not reveal where that mountain is.

Similarly, God directed Avraham Avinu, "Go forth from your land and from your birthplace and from your father's house to the land which I shall show you."[3] He did not tell him where he was supposed to go. In the same way, God commanded Avraham to take his son Yitzchak and to "offer him up as a sacrifice on one of the mountains which I shall tell you."[4] Here too, God did not, at first, reveal to Avraham exactly where that mountain was.

When it comes to momentous decisions, we are not always entirely sure where we're going when we start out. One who lacks faith, though, doesn't set out at all. We must take that initial step in the knowledge that only later will we understand where we are going. There are things which cannot be expressed in words – which are incomprehensible to human beings. Even if they are clearly articulated, they remain unfathomable. People may delude themselves into thinking they understand, but they don't. Therefore, it is pointless even to try to speak, and it is better not to reveal these secrets until the appropriate time comes, when they will be understood. Thus, when Avraham Avinu first set out from Ur of the Chaldees, the name *"Eretz Yisrael"* was not mentioned. So, too, the exact spot of *Akeidat Yitzchak* was also kept secret. In the same way, the name *"Yerushalayim"* was not mentioned in the Torah until the time came for King David to conquer it.

There is, however, one place in the Torah where Jerusalem does appear albeit obliquely: "And Malki-Zedek, King of Shalem...."[5] Shalem stands for Jerusalem. There are many ways to prove this. In *Tehillim*, it says, "And His *sukka* was in Shalem, and His dwelling place in Zion."[6] In this verse, "Shalem" parallels Jerusalem (Zion). There is also a reference in the Book of *Yehoshua* to "Adoni-Zedek, King of Jerusalem."[7] The word *Zedek* signifies the title of the king of Shalem-Jerusalem, just as the kings of Egypt were Pharaohs and the rulers of the Philistines were Avimelechs.

Obstacles in conquering Jerusalem

It was not easy for *Am Yisrael* to reach Jerusalem in the time of Yehoshua. Even though its king, Adoni-Zedek, was killed together with the other kings of the southern city-states,[8] the city itself was not conquered. This can be seen from the verse in *Yehoshua*, "And the Jebusites who dwelled in Jerusalem – the tribe of Yehuda could not drive them out. And the Jebusites have dwelled with the tribe of Yehuda in Jerusalem until this day."[9]

Neither was it a simple matter for King David to conquer the city, as we see from the verses in *Shmuel*:

> And the king and his men went to Jerusalem to the Jebusites, the inhabitants of the land, and they said to David, "You shall not come in here, unless you remove the blind and the lame," thinking that David would not come there. Nevertheless David captured the Fortress of Zion which is the City of David. And David said on that day, "Anyone who smites the Jebusites and gets up to the *tzinor*, and smites the lame and the blind whom David

hates with all his soul." Therefore it is said, "Neither the blind nor the lame shall come into the house."[10]

This passage is unintelligible. Who are the "blind and the lame," and how did they prevent David from entering Jerusalem? What is the *"tzinor"*? Many interpretations have been offered, from military, political and allegorical perspectives. The simplest explanation is that the city was so strongly fortified, and the Jebusites were so sure it was impregnable, that they mocked David, saying that even if they were defended by "the blind and the lame," he would not be capable of conquering the city. In the end, though, the city was conquered. David entered it through the *"tzinor,"* the aqueduct which brought water into the city. This is the literal explanation.

Our Sages interpreted "the blind and the lame" to be an allusion by the Jebusites to a peace pact made between Avimelech, king of the Philistines, and our forefathers.[11] According to this interpretation, "the blind" is a reference to Yitzchak (who was blind in his old age), and "the lame" is Yaakov (who limped as a consequence of fighting with the angel). Our Sages were critical of the non-aggression pact that our forefathers made because it brought about many tragedies in its wake.[12] David did not see himself as bound by this treaty since it had been blatantly breached by the Philistines themselves for several generations. Therefore, he was free to conquer the Fortress of Zion.

No matter which interpretation you choose, it is obvious that conquering Jerusalem was no simple matter, neither strategically nor politically. We, too, failed to hold onto Jerusalem in the War of Independence in 1948, despite all the numerous attempts made. We merited outstanding victories all over the country, but the battles in Jerusalem were accompanied by misfortune all along. Not until twenty years later, in the Six Day War, did we enter the gates of the city. The recurring difficulties we encountered in conquering Jerusalem reflect the air of mystery surrounding it in the Torah.

Malki-Zedek, King of Shalem

Returning from the battlefield after rescuing his nephew, Lot, from the four kings, Avraham met an outstanding individual – Malki-Zedek, King of Shalem. We are told: "Malki-Zedek, King of Shalem, brought out bread and wine, and he was a priest of the most exalted God, and he blessed

[Avraham], saying, 'Blessed is Avraham of the most exalted God, possessor of heavens and earth, and blessed is the most exalted God, who has defeated your enemies by your hands.'"[13] At this meeting, Avraham Avinu encountered a hospitable individual. Until now, he had always been the one to give to others, while they attempted to steal from him; now, finally, someone offered *him* something – bread and wine. In addition, this man blessed him in the name of "the most exalted God." He was a monotheist who believed in one God, the Creator and Ruler of the world. His name, "Malki-Zedek," or "King of Righteousness," was not his own personal name, but rather a royal title which expressed the essence of his kingship and of his city, Shalem or Jerusalem.

The bread and wine that Malki-Zedek gave Avraham are symbolic, just as Pharaoh's ministers, key figures in the story of Yosef, were the Chief Baker and the Chief Wine-bearer, and they dreamed about bread and wine.[14] Likewise, offerings of meal and wine are sacrificed on the altar in the *Beit HaMikdash*.[15] These are the staples of material and spiritual life. Malki-Zedek is a "priest of the most exalted God," the spiritual leader of his time. Our Sages identify him as Shem, son of Noach, as is written, "Blessed is God, the Lord of Shem."[16] At this meeting, Malki-Zedek presented the bread and wine to Avraham. According to our Sages, this was a symbolic transfer of spiritual leadership to Avraham.[17]

Malki-Zedek transfers leadership to Avraham

What did Malki-Zedek see in Avraham that caused him to relinquish his position of leadership to him? Possibly, it was Avraham's readiness to fight and to sacrifice everything for his ideals.[18] Perhaps it was also the noble, unselfish way in which he behaved during and after the battle with the four kings. Fighting a war did not transform Avraham into a cruel, greedy person, as so often happens to the best of men. Malki-Zedek realized that Avraham was a greater leader than he, and ceded the spiritual leadership of the priesthood to him.

Noach was also a righteous person. But when God warned him that there would be a flood, he accepted it silently, without protest. In contrast, when God told Avraham that He was about to destroy Sodom, Avraham argued, "Shall the Judge of the whole world not do justice?"[19] His sense of responsibility for mankind did not allow him to accept the decree passively.[20]

R. Menachem Mendel of Kotzk offered the following analogy: When you are cold, you have two choices – you can put on a fur coat and warm only yourself, or you can light a bonfire and provide warmth for others. Noach was the *tzaddik* with a fur coat, while Avraham lit a fire. He taught and cared for everyone. His goal was to redeem all of mankind from its physical and spiritual ills. Avraham was the biological father of *Am Yisrael*, but the spiritual father of the universe. He was therefore named "the father of a multitude of peoples,"[21] and all nations are blessed through him.[22] Thus, he was worthy of receiving the priesthood from Malki-Zedek, King of Shalem, the city of justice, at a time when the significance of Jerusalem was not yet revealed in the world.

Jerusalem as the center for the Jews and the whole world

At *Akeidat Yitzchak*, Avraham Avinu came to Mount Moria, the place where the *Beit HaMikdash* was destined to stand, and called it, "God will see (*Hashem yireh*), as it is said to this day, 'In the mountain God will be seen (*yeira'eh*).'"[23] On this mountain, we "see" God, and He "sees" us. The *Beit HaMikdash* has value aside from the sacrifices. It is called *Ohel Mo'ed*, a place of meeting and communication. This place, where all of *Am Yisrael* could be "seen" by God, was also the place where the worthy could merit the powerful spiritual experience of "seeing" God.[24] This special place enables us to reach a higher spiritual level than would be possible anywhere else. Thus, the first half of the name *Yerushalayim – yireh* – derives from Avraham and Yitzchak's *Akeida* experience on Mount Moria. The second half of *Yerushalayim – Shalem* – comes from "Malki-Zedek, King of Shalem."[25] Malki-Zedek, spiritual father of mankind, and Avraham Avinu, father of *Am Yisrael*, meet in Jerusalem, and it is named after both of them. Jerusalem is the capital of *Am Yisrael*, and is under their sovereignty, but it is also a "house of prayer for all nations."[26] It is the center for the Jews and for the whole world as well.

Christianity considers Jerusalem the center of the world. It doesn't matter to the Christians if Jews settle in Tel Aviv, but they must not do so in Jerusalem! The basis of the Christian faith is that *Am Yisrael* ceased to be the Chosen People because they killed "god" and were thus cast off. To them, Jews are relegated to being merely "Israel of the flesh," while Christians are now the true "Israel of the spirit" perpetuating the Jews' historic mission; it is they, therefore, who should return to Jerusalem. Today, we see with our own eyes that it is we – and not they – who have returned to Jerusalem. This is a fatal blow to Christian theology. Thus, we can understand their tremendous opposition to Israeli rule over Jerusalem.

In a similar manner, Moslems consider Jerusalem a holy city and universal spiritual center. Shortly after the Six Day War, a theological congress was held at El-Azhar University in Cairo, and a resolution was passed to fight to the last drop of blood for Moslem rule over Jerusalem, not on political or strategic grounds, but for religious reasons. This city is holy to them, and they see themselves as possessors of the true faith.

Jerusalem unites Am Yisrael

For *Am Yisrael*, Jerusalem is "built as a city that is joined (*chubra*) together,"[2] which our Sages explain is a city which "makes all of Israel friends (*chaver im*)."[28] This has halachic implications: *Am Yisrael* is divided into regular people, known as *amei ha'aretz*, and Torah scholars, known as *chaverim*. The *amei ha'aretz* are good people, but limited in their education and ideals,[2] whereas the scholars are holy, learned and idealistic people. The *am ha'aretz* is not as strict in the fulfillment of certain commandments, such as ritual purity and the separating of tithes. As a result, a gap exists between the two groups. However, at the time of the pilgrim festivals, when all of *Am Yisrael* ascended to Jerusalem, this division crumbled and all of *Am Yisrael* became *chaverim*. Jerusalem is the heart, the center of life, and there are, therefore no differing levels of holiness there. In addition, Jerusalem was not divided among the tribes,[30] but rather belonged to *Am Yisrael* as a whole.

Three times a year, on the pilgrimage festivals, all Jewish men would greet their God. At the end of the Sabbatical year, once every seven years, all men women and children would gather in Jerusalem for the *Hakhel* ceremony.[3] Everyone comes to "see" God; each merits a different spiritual experience according to his or her own spiritual level, but all are seen by God. At the same time, we see each other in all our varied forms of expression. We speak and exchange ideas, and this encounter enriches and unites all the individual members of *Am Yisrael*. All this takes place in Jerusalem, the city which has the ability to unite all of *Am Yisrael* as one – the city of love and peace.

There is a famous legend of two brothers, one poor and the head of a large family, the other wealthy but alone. In the middle of the night, the brother with the large family would secretly bring stacks of wheat over to his brother's field, saying, "My poor brother is all alone, let him at least take joy in his bountiful harvest." The other brother did the same, thinking, "My poor brother has so many mouths to feed, he needs much more than I do." They continued to bring wheat over to each other's fields at night until one night they met in the middle of the field and fell into each other's arms – and on that spot the *Beit HaMikdash* was later built.

There are those who talk about peace, referring to peace with the nations of the world. When the Torah talks about peace, however, it means peace among the members of *Am Yisrael*. Clearly, one does not preclude the other, but peace within our nation must take precedence.

Avraham Avinu received the priesthood – the responsibility for the spiritual welfare of mankind – from Malki-Zedek, King of Shalem, the city of justice. As "the father of a multitude of peoples," Avraham bears collective responsibility. As the children of Avraham, the Redemption we experience today has universal significance. We are called upon to build a just society which will serve as an example for the whole world. Despite our failures in the past, we, with our Jewish soul, are capable of doing this, and we will ultimately fulfill our mission. Today, we are still in the middle of the process; it is not yet time to build the *Beit HaMikdash*.[32] First, we must establish a sovereign *Eretz Yisrael*, i.e., a strong, prosperous and developed State. Only then will it be time to build the *Beit HaMikdash*. When the time is ripe, we will understand how to accomplish it. As we work our way towards this goal, that which is still a mystery today will become clearer and clearer, until Jerusalem finally becomes the universal center of justice.

Stones With a Human Heart

THE *KOTEL* STANDS tall and proud, armed with mightiness, emanating immortality. The historic saga of an eternal nation is bound up in her very stones. This is the heart of our nation, the place where all "the tribes went up,"[33] where all hearts turned towards Heaven.

Am Yisrael began as a group of persecuted individuals in Egypt. After gaining their freedom, they formed a nation and began the long journey towards their homeland. They struggled for centuries, finally building a kingdom and establishing Jerusalem as the capital, and in its heart, the Temple Mount – light of the whole world.

Alas, *Am Yisrael* sinned; we lost our kingdom and our *Beit HaMikdash.* But not completely: a token of Zion's former glory survives, for the Divine presence has not departed from the *Kotel.* The Wall of Tears remains etched in every heart and soul, imbued with all the hopes and beliefs in the impending restoration of our former glory.

Every Jewish person studying Torah holds a book bearing a picture of the *Kotel.* Everyone who pours out his or her heart to God lovingly strokes a bronze engraving of the *Kotel* on the *siddur.* The famous verse in *Tehillim* declares, "If I forget you, O Jerusalem, let my right hand forget its cunning."[34] The Jews of *Eretz Yisrael,* the survivors, flock to the *Kotel,* smothering it with kisses and drenching it with tears, whispering to it their innermost secrets.

The cruel enemy who laid waste our Land sought to deny us this last tangible symbol of our hopes and dreams. Pious Jews who approached the *Kotel* with reverence and awe were spat upon, stoned and stabbed, and the precious stones were smeared with excrement.

A brave Jew who hid a *shofar* under his shirt and blew it at the *Kotel* was arrested by the foreign occupier. But this sound – the sound of our freedom and of the ingathering of the exiles – cannot be silenced. Now the time for this sound has come. From all corners of the world, Jews return to their Land, and they are drawn to the *Kotel* as if to a magnet.

Am Yisrael has returned to *Eretz Yisrael*, and neither Pharaohs nor pogroms were able to stop us. We are rooted in this Land, wedded to it by blood. And *Eretz Yisrael* responded in kind to our love, blessing us with an abundance of produce. Step by step, Zion was rebuilt, Jewish fighters rose from the ashes of history, *Am Yisrael* regained its freedom and the State was born. The famous chapter of *Tehillim* foretells:

> When God returns us to Zion, we are as if in a dream. Then our mouths fill with laughter and our tongues with joy. Then the nations of the world shall say: "God has dealt wondrously with them." God has indeed dealt wondrously with us, and we rejoice. O God, return our exiles like the streams in the Negev [which fill up instantaneously after a flash flood]. Those who sow in tears shall reap in joy. He who goes weeping on his way, bearing a bag of seed, shall joyfully return, carrying his sheaves of wheat.[35]

Nevertheless, a cloud darkened the sky. Our book of life was missing its main chapter. Where is the heart? Where is the *Kotel*? We declared, "If I forget you, O Jerusalem, let my right hand forget its cunning. Let my tongue cleave to my palate if I do not mention you, if I do not raise Jerusalem above my greatest joy." Another upheaval for *Am Yisrael*: After nineteen long years, we returned to the Old City of Jerusalem. Soldiers of the Israeli Defense Forces kissed the stones of the *Kotel*, the weapons still warm in their hands.

As our Wall is to all other walls, so is *Am Yisrael* to the nations of the world. Our Wall was buried under garbage and refuse, yet it survived the ravages of time, while others were destroyed ten times over. Our Wall stands as tall and strong as ever, as does *Am Yisrael* stand strong once more. Mighty empires, scientific and cultural powers, rise and fall – but we are eternal.

The *Kotel* is a reflection of the generation. During the exile, it was a narrow hidden wall – accessible only through dark winding alleyways – a mirror of our anguish. Now that the light of our Redemption has begun to shine, the *Kotel* is shedding its squalor, rising to its full height, expanding in all directions, bathed in glory, open and expansive, as it radiates light over all of *Eretz Yisrael.*

R. Avraham Yitzchak Kook said, "There are all kinds of hearts. There are human hearts and there are hearts of stone. There are all kinds of stones. There are silent stones and stones with hearts. These stones are our hearts." At the *Kotel*, all hearts join together, all barriers between brothers disappear. The labels "religious" and "secular," "right" and "left," lose their meaning. We are all one nation with one heart. Says the verse in *Tehillim*, "Jerusalem is built as a city which is joined together."[36] Our Sages comment on this verse: "It is a city which joins all of Israel as one."[37]

Shavuot

Torah and Prophecy

The prophecies of Moshe Rabbeinu and the other prophets

"And never did a prophet arise in Israel like Moshe, whom the Lord knew face to face."[1] *Rambam*, listing the principles and fundamentals of our religion, states:

> The seventh principle concerns the prophecy of Moshe Rabbeinu, may he rest in peace. We are commanded to believe that he is the father of all the prophets who lived before him and who arose after him; they are all lesser than he in degree. He was the most chosen from all of mankind; he attained the knowledge of God more than any man in the past had and surpasses the potential of any man in the future.[2]

Why is it so important to emphasize that Moshe will never be surpassed? The answer is that if we were to accept the possibility that a prophet greater than he might arise, we might also think that such a prophet could replace the Torah that Moshe taught us. This possibility is inconceivable, because the Torah is eternal. For this reason, Moshe's prophecy is considered the highest level of all time.[3]

Moshe is not only the greatest of all the prophets, he is simply in a different league from all others. True, both Moshe and the others are called "prophets," but this is because no other word can adequately describe Moshe. Nor is there a unique term for Moshe's prophecy.[4] Yet this should not distract us from understanding the difference between the prophecies of Moshe and those of the other prophets.

The "brilliant glass" versus the "cloudy glass"

We are told that Moshe Rabbeinu saw through a "clear and brilliant glass," while the vision of the other prophets was not as lucid.[5] The prophetic vision of the other prophets is, of course, unambiguous and indisputable. If, for instance, Avraham had had the slightest doubt about God's revelation to him when he was commanded to bind Yitzchak to the altar, he never would have obeyed this order.[6] Still, Moshe's vision was inestimably clearer. When Yeshayahu the prophet said, "And I saw God,"[7] he was under the impression that he had actually seen God. In contrast, Moshe Rabbeinu, who had taught the Torah's words, "for no man will see me and live,"[8] knew that he could not truly see God.[9] Moshe's clarity came from the fact that he saw through a "clear glass."

Moshe's Torah and his vision are clear, detailed, precise, all-inclusive, appropriate for all generations and suitable for all situations.[10] The Torah is the soul of the entire world and its essential substance; it provides direction and imparts significance. In fact, the Torah preceded the world; it is the blueprint of the world and sets its agenda – i.e., it teaches us the way the world must be and the way it will be.[11] The Torah is the world's internal mechanism. Moshe Rabbeinu saw everything: all the general rules, all the specifics, all the times and places, all the circumstances of past and future.

Eternity and transience

Moshe's prophecy is called "Torah," while that of the other prophets is called "words of transmission." *Rashi* explains the difference: "The Torah was given to instruct all generations, whereas the prophets' words are only referred to as 'words of transmission,' because they received each prophecy from the Divine Spirit according to the needs of the time, the generation and the deeds themselves."[12]

The word Torah comes from *hora'a*, meaning instruction. It signifies education, method and absolute truth, eternal and everlasting.[13] Prophecy, on the other hand, is received only for specific situations, or for certain generations. It can be included in the category of "urgent provisional measures" – rules for exceptional, irregular circumstances. The Torah granted the prophets permission to issue temporary commands (except regarding idol worship), even against the Torah itself.[14] For instance, the prophet Eliyahu built an altar on Mount Carmel at a time when it was strictly forbidden to do so outside the *Beit HaMikdash*.[15] He only did this, of course, to safeguard the Torah.

Furthermore, we know that our forefathers Avraham, Yitzchak, Yaakov, and their descendants, fulfilled the Torah's commandments,[16] even though the Torah hadn't yet been revealed to *Am Yisrael*. Yet we find that there were times that they transgressed Torah laws, such as when Yaakov married two sisters, and when he built an altar,[17] and when Amram (Moshe's father) married his own aunt Yocheved.[18] How can this be? The answer is that they did not fulfill the Torah as "eternal Torah," but only as "prophecy," which consists of "temporary orders" that are appropriate for special situations.

Many prophecies were received and transmitted. The Talmud tells us that there were twice the number of prophets as people who left Egypt![19] Obviously, not all of what they prophesied was recorded and included in the Torah, except for that which was deemed to be "necessary for all time" – that which has significance beyond the generation in which it was given. The defining characteristic of prophecy, though, is that it is given only for a specific time. True, in exceptional cases, the same circumstances will repeat themselves, rendering a particular prophecy "necessary for all time." But the principle remains valid: Torah is eternal; prophecy is transient.

Halacha and universal morality

As we have said above, Moshe sees through a "clear and brilliant glass." His vision extends to even the smallest details, and thus his prophecy deals with precise, practical laws. The other prophets, however, see through a "cloudy glass." Their view encompasses the big picture and addresses overall principles of what is right and just. Their vision is not sufficiently penetrating to see how these principles diverge into the myriad of particular, intricate laws which constitute *Halacha*.

The Christians rejected the Torah because its obligations were too delineated and specific for their taste: this is permitted, that is forbidden, this is obligatory, etc. They repudiated the *mitzvot*, but they were drawn to the words of the prophets who spoke in general terms: "Seek justice, relieve the oppressed...."[20] These were undefined moral obligations that could be interpreted in various ways and do not obligate one to carry out particular actions. But the Torah of Moshe includes both the general, exalted principles and their practical, defined and obligatory details.

Comprehensive Torah and partial Torah

Every sage in *Am Yisrael* sees the Torah from his own viewpoint, according to his own understanding. All sages study the Torah, and it molds and shapes their ways of thinking – but each one has a "Torah mind" of his own. This diversity of thought allows for disagreement on certain points. Every Torah sage sees things differently from his fellow, and through his own "glasses." Where, then, is the Torah's truth? Which sage is teaching us what the Torah really means?

The answer is: all of them. The Talmud teaches us that, "The words of these sages and those – all are the words of the living God."[21] We must study the words of all of them: those who would rule something pure according to *Halacha*, and those who would rule it impure; those who would exempt, and those who would obligate; those who would permit, and those who would forbid.[22] Each of them represents a different aspect of the Torah, and they must all be seen together.

However, Moshe Rabbeinu is different. His words do not constitute just another "aspect." It's not that he saw things from one angle while others see things from another. Whoever sees things differently from Moshe is outside the framework of Torah! He becomes like Korach and his congregation, who differed with Moshe and consequently were swallowed up by the earth.[23]

Moshe represents the entirety of Torah. God said about him: "He is trusted throughout My entire house."[24] In addition, the Talmud teaches, "Anything that any veteran student will say before his teacher was already taught to Moshe at Sinai."[25] All of our studies are just an expansion upon that which Moshe already taught. Our Sages describe in the *Midrash* what happened when Moshe asked God to show him R. Akiva, the sage who derived detailed *halachot* from the very crownlets of the Torah's letters:

> God instructed Moshe: "Turn around." Moshe went and sat behind eight rows of Torah scholars studying under R. Akiva, and found that he did not understand what they were saying. He thereupon felt faint. At one point,

the students asked R. Akiva, "Rebbe, from where do you know this?" He answered, "It was taught to Moshe at Sinai [and handed down through the generations]." Moshe was relieved.[26]

This tells us that everything is included within the Torah of Moshe. Moshe learned and taught the principles in a general way, and their hidden details were expounded on, and revealed by, R. Akiva and the Sages throughout the generations.[27]

The prophets do not have students in the accepted sense of the word.[28] A person is either a prophet, or he is not. But Moshe has students who, deriving their strength from him, are able to develop his ideas into new ones. Moshe's concepts are so eternal and all-encompassing that students throughout the generations are able to pass them on and even extend them. Every generation faces new problems and circumstances which Moshe Rabbeinu did not have to contend with. As time passes, an ever-greater number of new issues manifest themselves. For each of these problems, a solution exists within the Torah, for the Torah is a Divine, everlasting, comprehensive doctrine, designed to help all of mankind – every nation, family and individual, in every time, place and situation. Those who engage in Torah learning are continuing the legacy of Moshe Rabbeinu, and are applying his words to new situations through elaboration, expansion, and the pinpointing of specifics therein. Every Torah student is called "Moshe"[29] – a little Moshe, a spark of Moshe Rabbeinu.

The Revelation at Sinai

Why was it necessary for the whole nation to experience the revelation at Sinai? Wouldn't it have been sufficient for Moshe Rabbeinu to simply transmit it to us? In order to answer these questions, we need to look into the Torah itself, where God says to Moshe, "Behold, I shall appear to you within the thickness of a cloud, so that the nation hears as I speak to you [Moshe], and they shall believe in you, too, forever."[30] It is vital that all of *Am Yisrael* received the Torah. The Ten Commandments that we received in public encompass all of the Torah, and since the whole nation witnessed the giving of the Torah, we have no need to prove the truth of our theology. *Rambam* states that *Am Yisrael* believed in the Torah and in Moshe Rabbeinu, not on account of the miracles, but because the nation itself heard the voice of God speaking:

> *Am Yisrael* believed in Moshe, not because of the miracles he performed, but because it was our own eyes, and not those of others, which witnessed the revelation at Sinai, and our own ears, and not those of others, which heard the fire and the thunder and the lightning, and Moshe entered the thick darkness [where the presence of God was], and the voice spoke to him and we heard: "Moshe, Moshe. Go and tell them...." Furthermore, the Torah says: "God spoke to you face to face...." How do we know that the revelation at Sinai is the sole proof that Moshe's prophecy is unequivocally true? Because the Torah says, "Behold I shall appear to you within the thickness of a cloud, so that the nation hear as I speak to you, and they shall believe in you, too, forever."[31]

After the first two commandments, *Am Yisrael* begged Moshe to intervene and transmit God's word to them, for they were not yet on a level where they could listen to God directly: "And they said to Moshe, 'You speak to us, and we shall listen; don't let God speak to us, lest we die.'"[32] On the one hand, it is essential to have complete faith in Moshe Rabbeinu. At the same time, it is vital for us to directly encounter our Creator, to realize that Moshe and his Torah are true, and that he speaks the word of God, so that the nation shall believe in Moshe forever. Thus, there were two elements present at Mount Sinai: the giving of the Torah through Moshe Rabbeinu, and the Divine revelation to the nation as a whole, which ensured that we unequivocally accepted the truth of the Torah. This wholehearted assurance is transmitted from one loyal Jew to the next through the generations. Whenever we study Torah, we reexperience the revelation at Sinai. For this reason, the Torah did not reveal exactly where and when it was given. Every day when we delve into the Torah, we express our connection to the revelation at Sinai.

Was the Torah Forced Upon Us at Sinai?

THERE SEEM TO BE two contradictory aspects to *Am Yisrael*'s receiving of the Torah. On the one hand, we learn in *parashat Yitro* that God compelled the nation by holding the mountain over them like a basin, saying, "If you receive the Torah, well and good, if not – this will be your grave!"[33] On the other hand, we see that *Am Yisrael* decided to accept the Torah out of free will: "The whole nation replied together and said, 'Everything which God has spoken we shall do.'"[34] Were *Am Yisrael* compelled to receive the Torah or did they accept it of their own free will?

It is essential to understand what the Talmud means by saying that God compelled *Am Yisrael* to receive the Torah. The world was created for the sake of the Torah; therefore, there is no validity to the world's continued existence without it. If the Torah had not been accepted, God would have returned the world to its original state of desolation and chaos. Creation requires the Torah, for it is the "Manufacturer's instruction manual." Not only did *Am Yisrael* have to accept the Torah for their own continued existence, but also for the purpose of keeping the whole world alive.[35]

God, who chose us, created us in such a way that we are a nation who desires the Torah. Just as we have no say in whether we want to be human or beast, so do we have no choice about whether we are born Jews or not. This is how we were formed, as "a nation who knows (i.e., has a close relationship with) its God." The upturned basin is not a case of coercion, but rather the emergence of a new reality with its own obligations. It is true that we still have the free choice of either living up to or denying our essence, but this potential cannot be changed. At Sinai, we were uplifted to a new level of consciousness, which brought the whole nation to the level of *"Na'aseh venishma,"* of identification with our inner essence. We realized who we were and what choices were necessitated by the new reality.

Receiving the Torah, however, is not just a one-time event; the Torah is given and received every day. This idea is reflected in the morning *beracha* we make on the Torah, which is phrased in the present tense.[36] The Torah is continually being given: God's word is perpetually in the process of being integrated into the world, becoming clearer and more comprehensible. At the time of *Matan Torah*, we had reached a certain maturity; we were saturated with human input and thirsted to hear the superhuman. There we received the Torah, but it was, to a certain extent, a forced acceptance, because the Torah did not harmonize completely with our spiritual status of the time. Thus, the acceptance was tinged with a hint of coercion; it was not completely compatible with our true selves. Thousands of years later, at the time of Purim, we accepted, once more, the Torah upon ourselves. Then, there was a renewed identification with the Torah, this time completely voluntary. As time passes, we are able to perceive that which was previously incomprehensible. This is our history – the increasing revelation of the letters of the Torah within ourselves.

The Fast of
the Seventeenth of Tammuz / Tisha B'Av

Confusion in the Dates of Destruction

THE SEVENTEENTH OF *TAMMUZ* marks the day on which the walls of Jerusalem were breached,[1] and has therefore been declared a fast day. However, the date itself is open to question, as the prophet Yirmiyahu writes, "In the fourth month, on the ninth of the month, the hunger in the city grew more severe, and the city was breached."[2] This indicates that the city walls were breached on the ninth of *Tammuz* rather than on the seventeenth. Rava, in the *Talmud Bavli*,[3] reconciles this contradiction by explaining that in the First Temple Period, the walls were indeed breached on the ninth, but in the Second Temple Period, they were breached on the seventeenth, and therefore the latter date was fixed as the date of fasting and commemoration.[4]

The *Talmud Yerushalmi* offers a different solution: "R. Tanchum bar Chanilai said, 'The dates here are miscalculated.'"[5] The city walls were indeed breached on the seventeenth, not on the ninth, but *Am Yisrael* endured such suffering during the period of destruction that they mixed up the dates. The prophecy was not corrected, but was recorded the way it was received at the time, to reflect the verse, "I [God] am with him [Israel] in his trouble."[6]

The *Talmud Yerushalmi* brings another example of the citation of a mistaken date, this time from *Yechezkel*: "And it was in the eleventh year, on the first day of the month, God spoke to me, saying, 'Son of man, since Tzor has spoken against Jerusalem, exclaiming: "Aha....."'"[7] Tzor probably rejoiced over the destruction of Jerusalem on the very day it was burnt down; it is only one day's journey from Jerusalem, and its people must have heard the news that same day. Accordingly, the destruction of the *Beit HaMikdash* occurred on the first of *Av*, which contradicts the accepted date of the ninth of *Av*. The same reasoning – that suffering caused the miscalculation of the dates – may explain this seeming contradiction as well. Both prophets erred in dating the terrible calamities: Yirmiyahu regarding the breaching of the walls and Yechezkel regarding the destruction of the *Beit HaMikdash*. This was due to their extreme grief over the devastation that was taking place.

We find various examples in the Torah which validate the saying that "troubles cause forgetfulness." According to our Sages, on the day that Moshe Rabbeinu died, 3,000 *halachot* were forgotten.[8] In a similar vein, *Rambam* explains how there came to be uncertainty about the sound of the *shofar*, whether it be *shevarim* or *terua*. In *Rambam*'s words: "Doubt arose due to the long period of exile, and therefore we don't actually know how the *shofar* should sound."[9] These cases illustrate how our troubles and worries have caused us to forget.

Can a prophet err?

Regarding theses dates – the seventeenth of *Tammuz* and the ninth of *Av* – such a theory is difficult to comprehend. After all, these dates are part of a prophecy. How can a prophet err while speaking in God's name? If he alters any part of the prophecy, he is a false prophet. How is it possible that a Divine message is inaccurate?

It is particularly difficult to understand how Yechezkel could have made such a mistake. Perhaps it is reasonable that in Jerusalem, in the midst of the havoc of battle and destruction, the Jews could have recorded a mistaken date. But Yechezkel, who prophesied in Babylonia – where the Jewish community lived in peace and security – saw the destruction only in his prophetic visions, so how could he have mistaken the date?[10]

The *Talmud Yerushalmi* attempts to deal with this difficulty by relating a parable: There was once a king who was sitting and tallying his accounts. In the midst of this, someone came and told him, "Your son has been abducted!" whereupon he lost count of all the figures. The king then declared: "From now on, I shall reckon all my accounts from this day!"

It would be unnatural if the king were not distraught when his son was abducted. Quite the opposite – in times of disaster, the natural order *is* disorder. Life cannot go on as usual. When the old order is destroyed, everything changes. This date marks the beginning of a new era.

There are other examples of "disorder" in the Torah. One is the principle that, "the Torah does not follow a chronological order,"[11] but rather a thematic order, which takes the form of combination of different *parshiot* or topics.[12] Events or ideas can be written in a place which seems historically inaccurate in order to convey an important message. Chronological order is not always the determining factor; rather, various needs and situations sometimes dictate other methods of sequence. Another example of disorder is the fact that miracles seem to violate the laws of nature, which represent order. *Maharal*, however, explains that they do not defy nature; they simply reflect an alternate system[13] which is of a higher order than the laws of nature to which we are accustomed in daily life.

The destruction of the *Beit HaMikdash* turned everything upside down and ushered in a terrible new reality. Our whole world collapsed, heaven and earth. The heavens ceased to be the same heavens: our connection to the Divine was weakened. Our Sages said, "Since the destruction of the *Beit HaMikdash*, heaven has not appeared in all its purity,"[14] as it is written: "I shall dress the heavens in darkness and clothe them in sackcloth."[15] Even the Divine light transmitted to us through our prophets was dimmed. Since the prophets are agents of the King – the Master of the World – it logically follows that disarray in the Divine connection to this world should manifest itself in disorderliness. A prophet is a person with receptors sensitive to the heavenly spheres of existence. When these spheres are in turmoil, it is expressed in a chaotic manner, and dates can be confused. The uncertainty regarding the dates was no incidental, technical mistake due to human error and forgetfulness. Rather, it reflects the cosmic state of destruction and confusion at the time of the prophecy.[16]

The Torah – the Five Books of Moshe – is eternal, not limited to any specific context. In contrast, the books of the prophets are termed "words of transmission," words spoken according to the need of the hour, the generation and the deed.[17] A prophet prophesies within a specific framework of time and place, according to the context within which the prophet lived. Does this in any way invalidate the prophecies? Of course not! All the words of the prophets are true,[18] but they must be understood as Divine guidance within the context of a specific circumstance, and therefore relevant only to that situation.

How can this idea be reconciled with the statement in the Talmud that "no prophecy was recorded unless it was relevant to all generations?"[19] The answer is that even though the confusion in the prophecy indicates that it was directed at that particular generation alone, it is still relevant for future generations and has much to teach us; otherwise it wouldn't have been written Obviously, the prophecy has no practical application in our days. However, it does teach us that when our national ethics have been corrupted, our political power is compromised, and we can no longer remain a sovereign entity. We must go into exile until we correct our moral failure.

God's word is transmitted to the prophet, and from him to the people in a manner suited to their particular situation. Just as a human king would lose track of all his accounts if his son were abducted, so do the prophets Yirmiyahu and Yechezkel "miscalculate" the date, which conveys to us the magnitude of the terrible sorrow they felt at the loss and destruction. The prophecy of the destruction reached Yirmiyahu and Yechezkel in a disorderly manner causing confusion in the date, for "the Torah speaks in human language."[20]

Does God cry over the destruction?

It says in *Yirmiyahu*, "My soul shall weep in secret (*mistorim*) for your pride."[21] The Talmud discusses this cryptic verse:

> R. Shmuel bar Onyo said in the name of Rav, "There is a place where God goes to cry, and its name is Mistorim." And what does "for your pride" mean? R. Shmuel bar Yitzchak said, "This refers to the pride of Israel which has been taken away from them and transferred to the other nations." But R. Shmuel bar Nachmani said, "This refers to the pride of the Kingdom of Heaven...."[22]

Here, the reaction to the destruction is presented as "crying." The Master of the World cries over the lost pride of *Am Yisrael*. Our national pride and strength has been shattered and violated. We were once an independent, respected State. At times we behaved well, and at others, not so well, but we were always able to hold our heads upright. Now, after the destruction, we have lost our independence and are broken and persecuted in exile. God must certainly cry over that.[23] Thus, two reasons are given for God's crying:

He is weeping over the Kingdom of Heaven and over the Kingdom of Israel. These two reasons are really one, for the Kingdom of Heaven only manifests itself in this world through the Kingdom of Israel. They are one.[24]

The Talmud asks: Can God really cry? The answer is: Outwardly, only strength and joy are evident, but inwardly, there is crying.[25] Similarly, even in exile, *Am Yisrael* rejoices over our communal life of Torah study and *mitzvot*, but inwardly we cry over our lost national pride. All the troubles and persecution we have suffered in the long years of exile came as a result of the destruction of the *Beit HaMikdash* and the Kingship. When the prophet Yirmiyahu describes the destruction in the last chapter of *Melachim*, he relates the fate suffered by King Tzidkiyahu, who was blinded after being forced to witness the slaughter of his sons, and then exiled to Babylonia. We know, though, that millions of Jews were murdered at the same time.[26] Why does Yirmiyahu depict only the king's torment, without mentioning the other victims? Because the entire tragedy came about as a result of the loss of sovereignty. Likewise in our time, the Holocaust could only happen when there was no sovereign State of Israel. Our lamentations on the Seventeenth of *Tammuz* and the Ninth of *Av* over the destruction of the *Beit HaMikdash* and the exile is really a mourning of the cause of all subsequent calamities. There is, therefore, no need to set aside a separate day of mourning for the Holocaust.[27]

Our Sages said: If the nations of the world only knew how good it would be for the whole world if the *Beit HaMikdash* were rebuilt in Jerusalem, they themselves would build it for us – of gold![28] In the same vein, we may say, "If the world only knew what a blessing it is for an independent Jewish State to exist, they would build us a state of gold." If they could recall all the justice and righteousness, all the ethical values and enlightenment bestowed upon the world by *Am Yisrael* in their own Land, and could understand that a return to our Land would introduce a new era for all mankind – they would lend us greater assistance and support.[29] But they do not understand this, so we must build the State by ourselves. This is the will of God.

Nevertheless, there have been a few righteous gentiles, such as Orde Wingate, who did understand. Wingate wrote that he was helping the Jewish people establish their own state despite the fact that this was contrary to the current interests of his British homeland, because he felt that all humanity would benefit from a sovereign Jewish State.

The Seventeenth of *Tammuz* denotes not only the breach made in the physical walls of the city, but also the breach made in Heaven. Since then, our world has been gloomy, weak and shaken. Today, thank God, the situation is being remedied. An independent State has been established and Jerusalem is in the process of being rebuilt. *Am Yisrael's* dignity is being restored. There is less hidden crying. At this point, it is irrelevant whether we have a monarchy or democracy, as long as we have our own sovereign State.[30] It may not be a perfect State, but it is certainly a completely different reality. We still cry inwardly over the Kingdom of Heaven that has not yet come, but we take comfort in the fact that we are only at the beginning stages. Eventually, the Kingdom of Israel will become the Kingdom of Heaven. We don't know how long it will take – perhaps hundreds of years – but we do know that it will happen, and we pray that it will happen in our lifetime.

Tu B'Av:
A Holiday of Unity and Joy

R. SHIMON BEN GAMLIEL TAUGHT: "Israel has had no holidays more joyous than Tu B'Av and Yom Kippur, when the young women of Jerusalem would go out...and dance in the vineyards."[1]

It is incredible that our Sages compared Tu B'Av – a holiday most people have never heard of – to Yom Kippur. What is so special about this day, the fifteenth day of the month of Av, which makes it deserving of such a noble comparison? We know that on Yom Kippur, Moshe Rabbeinu brought down the second set of Tablets to *Am Yisrael*, and God forgave *Am Yisrael* for the sin of the Golden Calf. Therefore this day – on which we received the Ten Commandments for the second time – has always been a day of forgiveness and rejoicing for us.[2]

There are six reasons given by the Talmud for us to rejoice on Tu B'Av:[3]

1 *On this day, the tribes were granted permission to marry one another.* When the first generation entered *Eretz Yisrael,* each tribe received their portion of land. Women who inherited their fathers' land were not allowed to marry out of their tribe, in order to keep the land within the same tribe. On Tu B'Av, the next generation of women was granted permission to marry whomever they desired, as the limitation on the first generation had expired.[4]

2 *The tribe of Binyamin was allowed to marry other tribes.* In the civil war following the incident of *Pilegesh BaGiva,*[5] the tribe of Binyamin was

almost wiped out, except for six hundred young men who managed to escape. *Am Yisrael* took an oath at Mitzpeh that they would not allow their daughters to marry anyone from the tribe of Binyamin. Later, when they realized that the tribe was in danger of extinction, they regretted the oath and looked for a way to allow the Binyaminites to marry and maintain themselves as a tribe. It was then decided that no one would initiate giving his daughter to a Binyaminite, but neither would he prevent them from marrying. These Binyaminites discovered where the girls of Shiloh went to dance, and "carried them off," with the tacit agreement of the girls and their parents. Thus, the tribe of Benjamin was saved from extinction.

3　*The "Generation of the Desert" came to an end.* Following the Sin of the Spies, when *Bnei Yisrael* cried about entering *Eretz Yisrael,* the entire generation of Israelites who had left Egypt was sentenced to die in the desert. Every year, on the eve of the ninth of *Av,* Moshe Rabbeinu would command them, "Go out and dig!" They would go out of their desert camp, dig themselves graves, and sleep in them overnight. The next morning, a messenger would proclaim, "Let the living separate from the dead!" About 15,000 men would die that night; the others would return to the camp for another year. In the last year, the fortieth year, the same procedure happened, except that no one died. At first they thought that they had miscalculated the dates, so they slept in their graves the following night, too. This continued until the fifteenth of *Av,* when they finally realized that no more people would die, and they declared a day of celebration.[6] In addition, during all those years, God did not appear to Moshe Rabbeinu in prophecy, but rather communicated with him through the *Urim VeTumim.*[7] This is like a couple who are angry with each other, and resort to writing notes because they are not on speaking terms. On Tu B'Av of the fortieth year, God began to speak to Moshe Rabbeinu directly.

4　*Jews were permitted to worship at the Beit HaMikdash.* Yerovam ben Nevat, the first king of the breakaway Kingdom of Israel, feared that if Jerusalem, the political capital of the Kingdom of Judah, continued to also serve as the spiritual capital of all *Eretz Yisrael,* it would weaken his sovereignty, leading to his eventual downfall. Therefore, he set up border policemen to prevent anyone from the Kingdom of Israel crossing over into the Kingdom of Judah and going to the *Beit HaMikdash* in Jerusalem.[8] One of the last kings, Hoshea ben Ela, annulled this decree on Tu B'Av, and permitted pilgrimage to Jerusalem.[9] Although he was not known as one of the more righteous kings, this act of Hoshea was a remarkable one.[10] The quality of this act compensated in some measure for his other sins.

5   *Those who were killed at Beitar were buried.* At the end of the Bar Kochba Revolt, the Romans conquered the city of Beitar and murdered thousands of Jews, leaving their corpses strewn all over the ground. The Romans, bent on breaking the Jews' spirit, would not even allow them to bury their dead.[11] Nothing could demoralize the remaining Jewish soldiers more than the sight of their friends lying dead on the ground beside them.[12] In Beitar, the bodies miraculously did not decompose during the prolonged period before Tu B'Av, when they were permitted to be buried. Following that, the Sages added another blessing, known as *"hatov vehameitiv,"* to *Birkat HaMazon*, the Grace after Meals. *Hatov* (He who is good) relates to the miracle of the bodies' remaining intact, and *hameitiv* (He who does good) gives thanks for their burial.[13] This blessing was added to honor the memory of Bar Kochba's fighters. Whenever we eat bread we recite this blessing afterwards, as part of *Birkat HaMazon*, despite the fact that the revolt itself was unsuccessful and we suffered great losses.

6   *No more trees were cut down for use on the holy altar after Tu B'Av every year.* Only dried wood was used to fuel the holy altar, since fresh logs might have contained worms and would thus have been disqualified for use. After Tu B'Av, the days became shorter, and the sun was no longer strong enough to dry out freshly cut logs before worms could enter. Therefore, it was decided that from Tu B'Av onwards, no more trees would be cut down, and the day was named, "Axe-breaking day."[14] The term alludes to the fact that there was no longer any need for axes that year, since enough wood had already been cut for the altar to last until the following summer.

This latter item, too, is connected to the destiny of *Eretz Yisrael*. The Talmud tells us of the family of Salmai of Netofa:

Once, the wicked rulers [the Romans] passed a law forbidding Jews to bring logs for the altar in the *Beit HaMikdash*. They stationed guards at checkpoints along the main roads, just as [the Kingdom of Israel's] Yerovam ben Nevat had done, to prevent Jews from coming to the *Beit HaMikdash*. What did the God-fearing men of that generation do? They made ladders out of the logs, and carried them on their shoulders. When the guards asked them, "Where are you going?" they answered, "To bring down birds from the birdhouse down the road, using the ladders on our shoulders." As soon as they passed the checkpoint, they dismantled the ladders and brought the logs up to Jerusalem. These people deserve to be remembered as "*tzaddikim* of blessed memory."[15]

Even under threat and persecution, we remained faithful to Jerusalem and to the *Beit HaMikdash*.

All of the six incidents which took place on Tu B'Av relate to unity; on this day, different segments of *Am Yisrael* were united and showed their commitment to *Eretz Yisrael* and the *Beit HaMikdash*:

- Jews of different tribes were permitted to marry one another.
- The tribe of Binyamin was once again allowed to marry women of other tribes, thus saving them from extinction, despite the grave sin they had committed.
- The Generation of the Desert ceased to die, and the Sin of the Spies – of rejecting *Eretz Yisrael* – was forgiven.
- The border policemen preventing Jews of the Kingdom of Israel from coming to Jerusalem were sent away. As a result, the ties between the Kingdom of Israel on the one hand and the Kingdom of Judah and *Beit HaMikdash* on the other were reestablished.
- The corpses of Beitar were brought to burial, honoring the memory of those freedom fighters who gave their lives to establish a sovereign State with the freedom to worship God as they chose.
- Trees were no longer cut down to be burnt on the holy altar. The custom of donating logs affords another opportunity to illustrate the dedication shown by *Am Yisrael* to uphold the service in *Beit HaMikdash*, even during times of persecution.

Domestic harmony within the nation, and harmony between the nation and its land, are really one and the same, for *Eretz Yisrael* is the factor which unites *Am Yisrael*. In *Eretz Yisrael* we become one nation.[16] As the prophet Shmuel says, "Who can compare to your people, Israel, one nation in the Land."[17] Tu B'Av is the opposite of Tisha B'Av: In contrast to the baseless hatred that brought about the destruction of the *Beit HaMikdash* and the exile of our nation, the events commemorated on Tu B'Av reflect love and unity within our people, and our deep connection to *Eretz Yisrael* and the *Beit HaMikdash*.

Why did R. Shimon ben Gamliel say that there were no days more joyous than Tu B'Av and Yom Kippur? Because Tu B'Av is a day of renewal of ties among Jews, and likewise Yom Kippur is a day of renewal of our ties to God. Yom Kippur is considered the wedding between *Am Yisrael* and God.[18] This is the time when God's wrath over the sin of the Golden Calf was appeased and Moshe Rabbeinu brought down the second Tablets to *Am Yisrael*. On this day we ask for forgiveness and "make peace" with God. We start afresh; our slate is clean.

There is a famous story about the Ba'al Shem Tov, who sent his disciples to learn how to repent by following the example of a very simple man. They saw him standing in prayer, holding two notebooks, and speaking to God: "Master of the Universe, in this notebook I have recorded the many sins which I have committed this past year. And in the other notebook, I have recorded all the suffering and troubles You have brought upon me. I will forgive You for all the suffering You have brought on me, if You forgive me for all my sins!" He then threw both notebooks into the fire. This should serve as a model for all our relationships – with our friends, our spouses, and so on. We must learn to throw all the notebooks into the fire, and begin anew.

Yom Kippur and Tu B'Av are, therefore, days of connection: between God and *Am Yisrael*; between Jews; and between Jews, *Eretz Yisrael* and the *Beit HaMikdash*. It is, therefore, fitting that on these days of spiritual unity, individual Jews should be married. We are now able to understand that, "Israel has had no holidays more joyous than Tu B'Av and Yom Kippur, when the young women of Jerusalem would go out…and dance in the vineyards [and choose their spouses]."

A Discussion of
Birkat HaMazon

WHAT CONNECTION is there between the tragedy of Beitar and *Birkat HaMazon*? Before answering this question, it is important to clarify how all the blessings of *Birkat HaMazon* relate to one another. R. Meir Simcha of Devinsk explains that the content of these blessings reminds us that the purpose of eating is to gather strength in order to strive on behalf of *Am Yisrael*. By reciting *Birkat HaMazon*, we sanctify the act of eating and channel the strength it gives us into spiritual, idealistic activity.

For that reason, our leaders composed these blessings: Moshe Rabbeinu, who sustained us in the desert for forty years, composed the first blessing, "Who sustains all life." Yehoshua, who brought us into *Eretz Yisrael*, composed the second blessing, which relates to *Eretz Yisrael*, *Brit Mila* and the Torah. King David and King Shlomo composed the third blessing, "Who builds Jerusalem." Each blessing is a step above the other: sustenance, then the Land, then Jerusalem and the *Beit HaMikdash*.[1]

The fourth blessing – composed by our Sages in honor of the dead of the Bar Kochba Revolt – represents a further stage: despite the traumatic defeat, we were not totally annihilated. Divine providence is particularly evident in the miraculous preservation of the corpses of Beitar until the time when they were finally buried. The Bar Kochba Revolt was but another phase in the battle over *Eretz Yisrael* and Jerusalem. Even though it ended in defeat, we will ultimately triumph.

Endnotes by Section

Rosh Hashana and Yom Kippur: The High Holy Days

1   *Avot* 4:2.
2   *Kohelet* 7:20.
3   *Mishlei* 24:16.
4   *Berachot* 34b.
5   *Pesachim* 54a.
6   *Tehillim* 84:8; *Berachot* 64a.
7   *Kohelet* 7:29.
8   *Chagiga* 12a.
9   *Bereishit* 1:11–12.
10 *Rashi* on *Bereishit Rabba* 5:9.
11 *Orot HaTeshuva* 4:2, 17:1.
12 *Yoma* 86a.
13 *Avot* 6:2.
14 *Devarim* 30:1–10.
15 Ibid., 1:8.
16 *Hilchot Teshuva* 7:1.
17 *Avot* 2:15.
18 *Hilchot Teshuva* 1:1.
19 *Bereishit* 3:12.
20 I *Shmuel* 15.
21 II *Shmuel* 12.
22 *Bereishit* 2:18.
23 *Rashi* op. cit.
24 *Avoda Zara* 17a.
25 R. Avraham Yitzchak Kook, *Orot HaTeshuva*, ch. 2.
26 *Orot HaKodesh* 3:302.
27 See introduction to *Orot HaTeshuva*.
28 *Mishlei* 24:16.
29 *Shemoneh Esrei*, *mussaf* of Rosh Hashana.
30 27:13.

31 The Hebrew root of *Ashur* denotes bliss. The root *osher* is found in *Bereishit* 30:13.

32 *Devarim* 32:15.

33 *Shemot* 6:9. The root of the word *Mitzrayim* is *tzar*, which means constriction.

34 *Hilchot Teshuva* 3:4.

35 *Orot HaChama*, cited by R. Margaliot in his commentary *Nitzotzei Ohr* on *Zohar Vayakhel* 203:2.

36 *Avot* 2:13.

Sukkot

1 *Tehillim* 76:3.

2 According to *Rema* in the *Shulchan Aruch*.

3 *Sukka* 11b; *Tur, Orach Chayim, siman* 4325.

4 *Devarim* 8:15–16.

5 *Bereishit* 31:40.

6 *Devarim* 8:3.

7 *Rambam, Guide to the Perplexed* 3:12.

8 Ibid., 3:24.

9 *Shemot* 14:11–12.

10 *Devarim* 8:16.

11 *Bamidbar* 9:23.

12 *Yeshayahu* 6:3.

13 Ibid., 43:7.

14 *Vayikra* 16:16; *Yoma* 56b–57a.

15 "The *Kohanim* could not stand to minister because of the cloud, for the glory of God had filled the house of God" (1 *Melachim* 8:11).

16 "And God said to Moshe: 'Behold, I come to you in the thickness of the cloud'" (*Shemot* 19:9); "And there was thunder and lightning and a thick cloud on the mountain" (19:16); "Moshe approached the thick darkness where God was" (20:18).

17 *Igrot HaRe'iya* 11, p. 334.

18 *Orot*, "*Yisrael U'Techiyato*" 1–2, pp. 18–19.

19 *Devarim* 4:4.

20 Ibid., 47:28.

21 *Hilchot Lulav* 8:15.

22 *Nidda* 61b.

23 R. Avraham Yitzchak Kook, *Orot HaKodesh* III, p. 129.

24 *Eiruvin* 100b.

25 *Yoma* 29b.

26 *Orot HaKodesh* III, p. 342.

27 *Devarim* 16:15.

28 *Sukka* 48a.

29 *Bamidbar* 21.
30 Outside of *Eretz Yisrael*, however, Shemini Atzeret and Simchat Torah are celebrated on separate days.
31 *Tiferet Yisrael*, ch. 1.
32 1 *Shmuel* 15:29.
33 *Yeshayahu* 44:5.
34 "Man sees with his eyes but God sees with His heart" (1 *Shmuel* 16:7).
35 44:21.
36 *Bechorei Yaakov*, as cited in *Mishna Berura, Orach Chayim* 669:9 par. 11.
37 11 *Shmuel* 6:14.

Chanuka: Contemplating Miracles

1   1 Maccabees 4:7–29.
2   See the section on Purim. Similarly, when Mordechai aroused Haman's fury by not bowing down to him, he was thought to be endangering the lives of all *Am Yisrael*.
3   1 Maccabees 4:30–31.
4   Ibid., 3:59.
5   From the *Al HaNissim* prayer.
6   *Mishpat Kohen*, p. 366.
7   1 Maccabees 2:32–44.
8   Ibid., 2:30,32–33.
9   See R. Kook's above quote that in times of religious persecution (*shemad*) a Jew has to give up his life rather than transgress a law of the Torah.
10 See R.M.T. Neria, "Permission to Fight on Shabbat, " *Torah SheBe'al Peh*, vol. 9, pp. 36–43.
11 *Devarim* 20:1–10; 1 Maccabees 3:56.
12 *Sota* 44b.
13 This situation is similar to that which took place in Israel at the time of the establishment of the State.
14 *Ner Mitzva*, p. 22.
15 *Me'iri*, commentary on *Shabbat* 21b; *Peri Chadash, siman* 670.
16 See *Tosafot, Bava Metzia* 106a.
17 R. Yosef Karo, *Maggid Meisharim, parashat Miketz*.
18 *Devarim* 17:15.
19 *Shabbat* 21b.
20 *Berachot* 20a.
21 1 *Shmuel* 17:34.
22 *Bava Metzia* 106a.
23 *Ta'anit* 25a.
24 *Esther* 10:3.

25 Ibid., 3:2: "For Mordechai the Jew would not kneel or bow."

26 *Shabbat* 88a on *Shemot* 19:17.

27 *Esther* 9:27.

28 1 *Maccabees* 3:59–60.

29 11 *Shmuel* 10:12.

30 *Ta'anit* 5a.

31 36:8.

32 *Sanhedrin* 98b.

The Holocaust

1 Recently published in English by Urim Publications.

2 *Tehillim* 118:5.

3 *Aish Kodesh, Derasha* for Rosh Hashana, 1939.

4 *Bereishit* 32:26.

5 *Sota* 34a.

6 *Parashat Vayishlach* 1941, p. 13.

7 Ibid., 1942, p. 137.

8 *Rashi* on *Bereishit* 1:1.

9 *Shemot* 5:22.

10 *Aish Kodesh, Shemini Atzeret* 1941, pp. 75–76.

11 *Sanhedrin* 98b.

12 *Berachot* 33b.

13 *Netivot Olam, Netiv Yirat Hashem.*

14 *Bereishit* 3:16.

15 66:9.

16 *Aish Kodesh, parashat Masei,* 1941.

17 R. Aviner is one of the founders of the Zvi Yisrael Institute for the Study of the Holocaust According to Jewish Faith.

18 Obviously, this did not exempt the Egyptians from responsibility, as *Rambam* explains in *Hilchot Teshuva* 6:5.

19 *Semachot* 8.

20 Ibid.

21 *Yerushalmi, Berachot* 1:1.

22 20:33–34.

23 *Yechezkel* 16:6.

Tu Bishvat

1 *Devarim* 13:5.

2 Ibid., 4:24.

3 *Bereishit* 2:8.

4   *Vayikra Rabba* 25:3.

5   *Sanhedrin* 24b; *Rambam, Hilchot Eidut* 10:4.

6   R. Avraham Yitzchak Kook, *Ikvei HaTzon*, "Da'at Elokim," p. 130.

7   Ibid.

8   R. Kook, *Igrot HaRe'iya*, vol. I, p. 164.

9   Ibid.

10 R. Kook, *Ma'amarei HaRe'iya, Aggadot Rabba bar Chana*, p. 438; *Shulchan Aruch* 231, *Mishna Berura* 8.

11 *Midrash Tanchuma, parashat Kedoshim* 8.

12 R. Kook, *Megged Yerachim, Shvat*.

13 R. Kook, *Orot*, "Orot HaTechiya" 16, p. 68.

Purim

1   As the prophet Yeshayahu said, "For the first persecutions will be forgotten and hidden from my eyes" (65:16).

2   *Hilchot Megilla* 2:9.

3   See *Chiddushei HaGriz* on *Rambam*.

4   *Yerushalmi, Megilla* 1:5.

5   *Ta'anit* 9b.

6   *Shabbat* 104a.

7   *Yeshayahu* 11:9.

8   *Yirmiyahu* 31:33.

9   *Derasha* 37, *Adar* 5592.

10 *Megilla* 16b.

11 *Esther* 9:30.

12 *Megilla* 1:5.

13 Ibid., 14a.

14 *Chullin* 137a.

15 See chapter in this book on Shavuot – "Torah and Prophecy."

16 *Nedarim* 22b.

17 3:22.

18 *Maharatz Chayos, Nedarim* 22a.

19 *Sefer HaMitzvot, Shoresh HaSheini*.

20 *Megilla* 14a.

21 *Ohr Chadash* 220 and see *Tiferet Yisrael*, ch. 53, and *Ohr Chadash* 47–49.

22 *Mishlei* 4:1 and 9:2.

23 *Midrash Shocher Tov, Mishlei, parasha* 9.

24 *Tikkunei Zohar, Tikkun* 21.

25 *Peleh Yoetz, Teruma*; Kalonymus Kalman Epstein, *Ma'or VaShemesh*; *HaAdmor MeRizin, Genizei Yisrael*.

26 No eating or drinking; no marital relations; no wearing of leather shoes; no washing or anointing the body.

27 *Esther* 9:1.

28 *Shelah HaKadosh* on *parashat Zachor*.

29 *Megilla* 7b.

30 *Aguda* quoted by *Darchei Moshe*; *Bach* on *Tur, Orach Chayim* 695.

31 *Berachot* 31b.

32 *Rambam, Hilchot Tefilla* 4:17.

33 *Eiruvin* 65a.

34 Ibid., 65b.

35 *Megged Yerachim, Ma'amarei HaRe'iya*, p. 501.

36 *Megilla* 12b.

37 *Berachot* 8b.

38 See *Me'iri*, cited in *Biur Halacha*, 695:2.

39 *Eiruvin* 65a.

40 *Olat Re'iya*, vol. 1, pp. 439–40.

41 See *Derech HaShem*, part 4, 7:6.

42 *Shabbat* 88a. See the chapter in this book on Shavuot – "Was the Torah Forced Upon Us at Sinai?"

43 *Shabbat* 88b.

44 See *Sefat Emet* on Purim, *Shemot* 90.

45 *Eicha* 1:9, a reference to Jerusalem at the time of the destruction.

46 *Vayikra* 16:16.

47 *Yoma* 56b–57a.

48 *Avot* 3:14.

49 *Eicha* 2:6.

50 *Yoma* 85b. This is the opinion of R. Yehuda HaNassi.

51 *Shut HaRashba* 1:93.

52 See *Radak* to 1 *Shmuel* 15:29.

53 *Esther* 3:13.

54 *Tehillim* 136:23–24.

55 *Yerushalmi, Kiddushin* 4:1.

56 Heard from R. Zvi Yehuda Kook.

57 *Esther* 9:1.

58 Introduction to the *Zohar* 4:1.

59 This is reflected in the fact that the two Hebrew terms "blessed be Mordechai" and "cursed be Haman" have the same numerical value.

60 *Keritot* 6b.

61 *Esther* 3:2

62 *Esther Rabba* 6:2, 7:8; *Torah Temima*.

63   *Aggadat Esther* 3:2; *Megilla* 12:2, commentary of *Radvaz.*
64   *Esther* 3:3,4.
65   Ibid., 3:5.
66   *Pesachim* 64b.
67   *Berachot* 7b.
68   *Bereishit* 33:3.
69   *Esther Rabba* 7:9.
70   *Ramban* on *Bereishit* 32:4.

Pesach

1   "No *chametz* should be seen or found" (*Shemot* 12:19, 13:17); *Igrot Moshe, Orach Chayim* 1 145; *Mishna Berura; Chazon Ish.*
2   *Chametz* that has been in a Jew's home over Pesach – but was sold – may be eaten after Pesach. *Mishna Berura, Sha'ar HaTziyun* 451:6; *Chazon Ish, Orach Chayim* 3117:15; *Mishna Berura* 142:33.
3   Responsa *Yechaveh Da'at* 5:149.
4   Crumbs alone may not be sold, for they have no halachic value. However, it is possible to sell all the food in a cabinet, which includes the *chametzdik* dirt inside.
5   *Orach Chayim* 433:11.
6   *Berachot* 20a.
7   *Malachi* 3:23.
8   *Pesikta Rabbati* 35.
9   Commentary of *Ravad* at the end of *Eiduyot.*
10   *Tzidkat HaTzaddik* 218.
11   *Sanhedrin* 32b.
12   Just as *Kesef Mishneh* is *Rambam*'s "right-hand man" – see *Rambam, Hilchot Melachim* 11:3.
13   See also R. Zvi Yehuda Kook, commentary on the Pesach *Haggada*, p. 39.
14   *Bamidbar* 24:17, cited in *Yerushalmi, Ta'anit* 4:5; *Eicha Rabba* 2:4.
15   *Yerushalmi,* ibid.
16   11:2–3; *Sanhedrin* 93b; *Ravad, Hilchot Melachim* ibid.
17   *Radvaz,* ibid.
18   *Eicha Rabba,* ibid.
19   *Rambam,* ibid.
20   R. Zvi Yehuda Kook, ibid., pp. 34–37.
21   He supported the Bar Kochba Revolt, treating it as if it were the Redemption (*Rambam,* ibid).
22   *Ma'amarei HaRe'iya* 202–203.
23   *Sefer Yetzira,* ch. 1.
24   *Avot* 5:1–6.

25 66:8.

26 Ibid., verse 9.

27 *Mishna Pesachim* 10.

28 The *Haggada*.

29 R. Avraham Yitzchak Kook, *Siddur Olat Re'iya*, vol. ii, p. 262.

30 20:8.

31 *Chullin* 7a.

32 According to *Sefer HaChinuch*, *Mitzva* 546, the greatest *tzaddikim* are above the laws of nature.

33 *Ta'anit* 25a.

34 *Mechilta* cited in *Rashi* on *Shemot* 15:2.

35 *Chullin*, ibid.

36 *Sichot HaRav Zvi Yehuda*, Lag B'Omer.

Yom HaAtzmaut: The Birth of a Jewish State

1 *Berachot* 34b.

2 *Hilchot Melachim* 12:2.

3 Many more prophecies have yet to be fulfilled, for example, "There shall be no needy among you" (*Devarim* 15:4) – that poverty will no longer exist in the End of Days. However, we are told that in the Messianic period, "Poverty will not disappear from the land" (*Devarim* 15:11) – that there will still be a gap between the rich and the poor. In *Berachot* 34b, Shmuel used this latter verse to prove that the only difference between the Messianic period and his generation was political independence. Therefore, the first verse, "There shall be no needy among you," must refer to a stage after the Messianic period.

4 *Hilchot Teshuva* 7:5 relating to *Devarim* 29:8.

5 *Bereishit* 1:31.

6 *Avot* 5:2–3.

7 *Bereishit* 12:2.

8 *Devarim* 11:31.

9 *Ramban*, Annotations to *Rambam*, *Sefer HaMitzvot*, Positive *Mitzva* 4.

10 *Ramban*, ibid.

11 There are other *mitzvot* that are the obligation of *Am Yisrael* as a whole, e.g., appointing a king, building the *Beit HaMikdash* and declaring war.

12 *Ramban*, ibid.

13 *Berachot* 32b.

14 *Yehoshua* 1:6,7,9,18.

15 *Hilchot Melachim* 5:9–12.

16 Ibid., 1:6.

17 *Sanhedrin* 49a; *Hilchot Melachim* 3:8.

18 *Yehoshua* 1:18.
19 National leaders are only granted kingly powers regarding the leadership of the nation and do not have the special dispensations granted to kings such as permission to marry eighteen wives, and so on.
20 See *Mishpat Kohen*, pp. 128, 365.
21 *Shulchan Aruch, Orach Chayim* 4161.
22 *Beit Yosef* on the *Tur, Orach Chayim*, ibid. Cited in the *Magen Avraham* and the *Mishna Berura*.
23 *BeMa'aracha HaTzibburit*, p. 55.
24 *Zecharia* 8:19.
25 *Rosh Hashana* 18b.
26 Both opinions are cited in the *Beit Yosef* on the *Tur, Orach Chayim* 415.
27 *Rambam, Commentary on the Mishnayot, Rosh Hashana* 1:3.
28 Ibid.
29 *Bereishit* 8:11.
30 *Eiruvin* 18b.
31 From the blessing recited before performance of a *mitzva*.
32 See further *Kiddushin* 31a; *Yam Shel Shlomo, Bava Kama* 7:37.
33 *Shemot* 6:6–8.
34 Ibid., 12:11.
35 Ibid., 15:20 and *Rashi* op. cit.
36 Ibid., 15:13.
37 See *Rambam, Hilchot Chanuka* 3:1: "And sovereignty returned to Israel for over 200 years."
38 *Shemot* 19:5–6.
39 1 *Melachim* 10:1–13.
40 *Maharal, Netzach Yisrael*, ch. 1.
41 36:16–20.
42 Ibid., 36:23–32.
43 *Rashi* on *Shemot* 13:18: "and '*chamushim*' did *Bnei Yisrael* leave the land of Egypt."
44 *Shir HaShirim* 5:2.
45 See *Targum* op. cit. and *Kuzari* 2:24.
46 *Nechemia* 7:66.
47 *Pesachim* 114b.
48 See *Sedei Chemed*, vol. iv, p. 306; *Beit Yosef* on *Orach Chayim*, par. 589.
49 See *Shulchan Aruch, Orach Chayim* 475:4, R. Teichtal, *Eim HaBanim Semeicha* (Urim Publications), p. 77; R. Yisrael of Kotzk, *Shalom L'Yerushalayim*, p. 7, *siman* 2; article of *Aderet* in the anthology *Shivat Zion*, p. 62; R.S. Mohilever op. cit. p. 7.
50 Commentary of Vilna Gaon to *Tehillim* 76:3, from *Kol HaTor*, ch. 1, par. 7.
51 36:25–26.
52 *Berachot* 1:1.

Lag B'Omer

1   *Yevamot* 62b.

2   *Shulchan Aruch, Orach Chayim* 493:1.

3   *Vayikra* 19:18.

4   *Yerushalmi, Nedarim* 9:4.

5   Pano, Ten Articles, article on *Eim Kol Chai*, pp. 1–3.

6   *Bamidbar* 25:1–9.

7   For example, it is prohibited to have your hair cut by a pagan, lest he kill you (*Avoda Zara* 29a; see further *Rambam, Hilchot Rotzai'ach U'Shmirat HaNefesh* 12:7–13). The monotheistic religions that were influenced by Judaism looked upon violence unfavorably. Jesus taught his disciples to "turn the other cheek" when attacked – but the Church itself found ways to legitimize the spilling of blood in order to battle the enemies of their lord.

8   *Bereishit* 34:25.

9   *Hilchot Melachim* 9:14.

10   *Bereishit* 48:5–7.

11   *Shemot* 32:26–29

12   *Devarim* 33:8–11.

13   *Hilchot Sanhedrin* 24:9.

14   R. Avraham Yitzchak Kook, *Orot*, "*Orot HaTechiya*" 45, p. 85.

15   *Shemot* 20:5–6.

16   *Yerushalmi, Nedarim* 9:4.

17   *Bereishit Rabba* 63:3.

18   *Igrot HaRe'iya* 1, pp. 320–21.

19   The term, "*gilgul neshamot*," or "reborn souls," may be understood as expressing the continuity of generations. We will not go into it any further here, particular as *Arizal* explains that this concept cannot be understood literally and is open to misinterpretation.

20   From the responsa of the *Geonim*, siman 362.

21   *Pesachim* 49b.

22   *Bechorot* 58a.

23   II *Melachim* 2:23–24.

24   *Sanhedrin* 109b.

25   See *Orot*, "*Eretz Yisrael U'Techiyato*" 15, p. 32.

26   *Sefer Hayuchasin*; *Rambam*, introduction to *Yad HaChazaka*.

27   See R.Y. Heinemann, *Toldot HaTannaim VeHaAmoraim*, on R. Akiva (*Gittin* 57b).

28   *Sanhedrin* 32b.

29   *Bereishit* 25:29.

30   *Bava Batra* 16b.

31   4:31.

32 *Bereishit* 27:40.

33 *Esther* 3:13.

34 *Devarim* 25:19.

35 *Middot HaRe'iya*, "*Ahava*" 6.

36 *Middot HaRe'iya*, "*Kavod*" 8–9.

37 Introduction to *Ha'amek Davar* on *Bereishit*.

38 *Shulchan Aruch, Orach Chayim* 493.

39 Ibid.

40 *Eiduyot* 2:10.

41 "On Pesach – grain, and on Shavuot – fruit" (*Mishna Rosh Hashana* 1:2).

42 Similarly, the Talmud tells us that childbirth, being a time of danger for a woman, is
    considered a time of judgment. A woman who has transgressed the three *mitzvot* for
    women (*nidda*, candlelighting and taking *challa*) can be sentenced to death by God at
    this time (*Shabbat* 31b).

Yom Yerushalayim

1 *Devarim* 12:5.

2 *Shemot* 15:17.

3 *Bereishit* 12:1.

4 Ibid., 22:2.

5 Ibid., 14:18.

6 *Tehillim* 76:2.

7 10:1.

8 Ibid., 10:26.

9 Ibid., 15:63.

10 II *Shmuel* 5:6–8.

11 "Avimelech said to Avraham: 'Swear to me…that you will not deal falsely with me, my
    great-grandson, and my grandson'" (*Bereishit* 21:22–34). *Rashi* brings a *midrash* which
    says that the Jebusites were descendants of Avimelech.

12 See *Rashi* op. cit. and *Pirkei DeRabbi Eliezer* 36.

13 *Bereishit* 14:18.

14 Ibid., 40. See also *Tehillim* 104:15.

15 *Rambam, Hilchot Ma'asei HaKorbanot* 2:1.

16 *Bereishit* 9:26.

17 *Nedarim* 32b.

18 *Itturei Torah, Bereishit*, p. 102, in the name of R. J.B. Soloveitchik.

19 *Bereishit* 18:23–33.

20 See *Zohar* 58:67b; *Igrot HaRe'iya* II, p. 188.

21 *Bereishit* 17:4,5.

22 Ibid., 12:3.

23   Ibid., 22:14.
24   See *Rambam, Hilchot Beit HaBechira* 1:1.
25   *Bereishit Rabba* 56:14.
26   *Yeshayahu* 56:7.
27   *Tehillim* 122:3.
28   *Yerushalmi, Chagiga* 3:6.
29   See *Tosafot* to *Pesachim* 49.
30   *Yoma* 12a.
31   *Devarim* 34:23; 31:10–13.
32   See *Rambam*, ibid., 1:1–2.
33   *Tehillim* 122:4.
34   Ibid., 137:5.
35   Ibid., 126. We recite this before *Birkat HaMazon* on Shabbat and Festivals.
36   Ibid., 122:3.
37   *Yerushalmi, Chagiga* 3:6.

Shavuot

1   *Devarim* 34:10.
2   Introduction to *Perek Chelek* of Tractate *Sanhedrin*. See also *Hilchot Yesodei HaTorah* 7.
3   *Bamidbar* 12:6; *Rambam, Ikkarei Emuna*, 7; R. Avraham Yitzchak Kook, *Siddur Olat Re'iya*, p. 334.
4   *Rambam, Guide to the Perplexed* 2:35.
5   *Yevamot* 49b.
6   *Rambam*, ibid., 3:24.
7   6:1.
8   *Shemot* 33:20.
9   *Yevamot* ibid., and *Rashi* op. cit.
10   *Bamidbar Rabba* 23:4: "God showed Moshe everything that was and that will be."
11   *Bereishit Rabba* 1.
12   *Chullin* 137a.
13   R. Kook, *Siddur Olat Re'iya*, pp. 159–160.
14   *Rambam, Hilchot Yesodei HaTorah* 9:3.
15   *Sanhedrin* 89b.
16   *Yoma* 28b.
17   *Bereishit* 28:18.
18   *Shemot* 2:1, *Sota* 12a.
19   *Megilla* 14a.
20   *Yeshayahu* 1:17.
21   *Eiruvin* 13b.
22   *Chagiga* 3b.

23 *Bamidbar* 16.

24 Ibid., 12:7, R. Kook, *Orot HaTorah* 1:1.

25 *Vayikra Rabba* 22:1. See also *Nidda* 45a and *Berachot* 5a.

26 *Menachot* 29b.

27 *Maharal, Tiferet Yisrael* ch. 63.

28 See *Hilchot Yesodei HaTorah* 7:45.

29 *Shabbat* 101b.

30 *Shemot* 19:9.

31 *Rambam, Hilchot Yesodei HaTorah* 8:1.

32 *Shemot* 20:16.

33 Ibid., 19:17. The verse tells us that the nation gathered "underneath" the mountain. *Rashi* op. cit. cites the Talmud, *Shabbat* 88a, which explains the idea of compulsion.

34 Ibid., 19:8.

35 *Maharal, Tiferet Yisrael*, ch. 32.

36 "Blessed is God who *gives* the Torah." See commentary of *Taz* on *Shulchan Aruch, Orach Chayim* 57, note 5.

The Fast of the Seventeenth of Tammuz / Tisha B'Av

1   *Mishna Ta'anit* 4b.

2   *Yirmiyahu* 52:6–7; 39:2; II *Melachim* 25:3–4.

3   *Ta'anit* 28b.

4   *Rosh Hashana* 18b, *Tosafot* op. cit.

5   *Yerushalmi, Ta'anit* 4:5.

6   *Tehillim* 91:15 and commentary of *Korban HaEida* to *Yerushalmi*, ibid.

7   26:1–2.

8   *Teruma* 16a.

9   *Hilchot Shofar* 3:2.

10 *Shiurei HaKorban* on *Yerushalmi* op. cit.

11 *Pesachim* 6b.

12 *Bava Kama* 107a: "A verse from another *parasha* has been inserted here and is out of place."

13 *Gevurot Hashem*, p. 7 of the second introduction.

14 *Berachot* 59a.

15 *Yeshayahu* 50:3.

16 See *Sichot* of R. Zvi Yehuda Kook on the Seventeenth of *Tammuz*, p. 1.

17 *Chullin* 137a and *Rashi* op. cit.

18 This is the sixth of *Rambam's* Thirteen Principles of Faith.

19 *Megilla* 14a.

20 *Berachot* 31b; see also R. Avraham Yitzchak Kook, *Eder HaYakar*, pp. 37–38.

21 13:17.

22 *Chagiga* 5b.

23 Of course, the above is a parable. We understand nothing about God: "They imagined You, but not as You really are, so they pictured You through Your deeds" (*Shir HaKavod*). We can only relate to God through human visualization, using the kind of language which would be appropriate for human beings. See the section "Tu Bishvat."

24 *Tanna D'vei Eliyahu Rabba* 4; *Mesillat Yesharim*, end of ch. 19.

25 *Chagiga* ibid.

26 *Gittin* 57b.

27 See R. Avraham Yitzchak Kook, *Orot*, "War."

28 *Bamidbar Rabba* 3a; *Netzach Yisrael*, ch. 5.

29 See *Igrot HaRe'iya* vol. III, no. 832.

30 Responsa *Mishpat Kohen* pp. 337–38; 378.

Tu B'Av: A Holiday of Unity and Joy

1   *Mishna Ta'anit* 4:8.

2   See *Rashi* on *Ta'anit* 28:2.

3   *Bava Batra* 121a.

4   Unfortunately, today we still suffer from tribal jealousy, and there are still Jews who consider it a tragedy if their offspring marries a Jew from another ethnic group.

5   See *Shoftim* 19:20.

6   *Yerushalmi, Ta'anit* 4:6. The reason they had not realized that the forty years were up was that they mistakenly counted forty years from the Sin of the Spies, while actually, the year they left Egypt was counted as the first year of the decree.

7   *Ta'anit* 30:2.

8   I *Melachim* 12.

9   II *Melachim* 17.

10 See *Rashi* on *Ta'anit* 31:1.

11 *Gittin* 57–58; *Ta'anit* ibid.

12 This is akin to what Israeli soldiers experienced during the Yom Kippur War.

13 *Berachot* 48b.

14 *Ta'anit* 31a; *Rashi* op. cit.

15 Ibid., 28a.

16 *Zohar, parashat Vayikra* 93b; *Netziv, Shivat Zion* vol. II; *Eim HaBanim Semeicha*, p. 321.

17 II *Shmuel* 7:23.

18 *Ta'anit* 26b.

A Discussion of *Birkat HaMazon*

1   See *Meshech Chochma* to *Devarim* 8:10; R. Avraham Yitzchak Kook, *Siddur Olat Re'iya* I, pp. 361–63.